Pushkar
The Paradise

A Photo Travelogue

By

PULKIT JOSHI

ISBN: 1512016829
ISBN-13: 978-1512016826

DEDICATION

To my family and friends

CONTENTS

ACKNOWLEDGMENTS

To people I met at the Pushkar Fair

INTRODUCTION

The Pushkar Fair (Pushkar Camel Fair) or locally Pushkar ka Mela is an annual five-day camel and livestock fair held in the town of Pushkar in the state of Rajasthan, India. It is one of the world's largest camel fairs. The fair is spread over a large area with camels and more camels all over the place. A perfect place to witness the traditional Rajasthani culture, it's very likely you will get swayed away by the fair in no time. With close to 50,000 to 60,000 camels and quarter million people attending this large fair, it's a visual treat. During the course of this fair, nearby farmers come together to trade their cattle, horses and camels. This travelogue is a collection of photographs taken during the last Pushkar Fair which started in the month of November, 2014. Thank you!

1. THE USUAL SUSPECTS

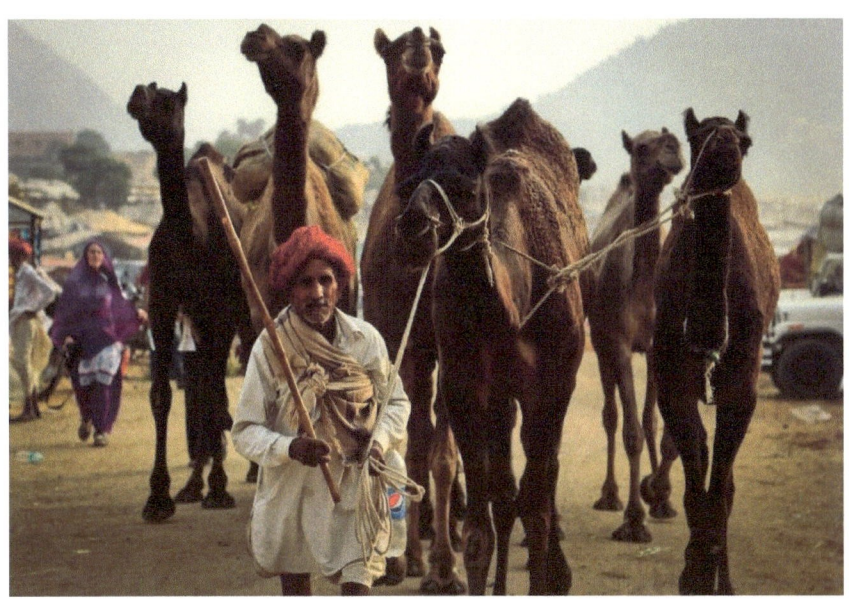

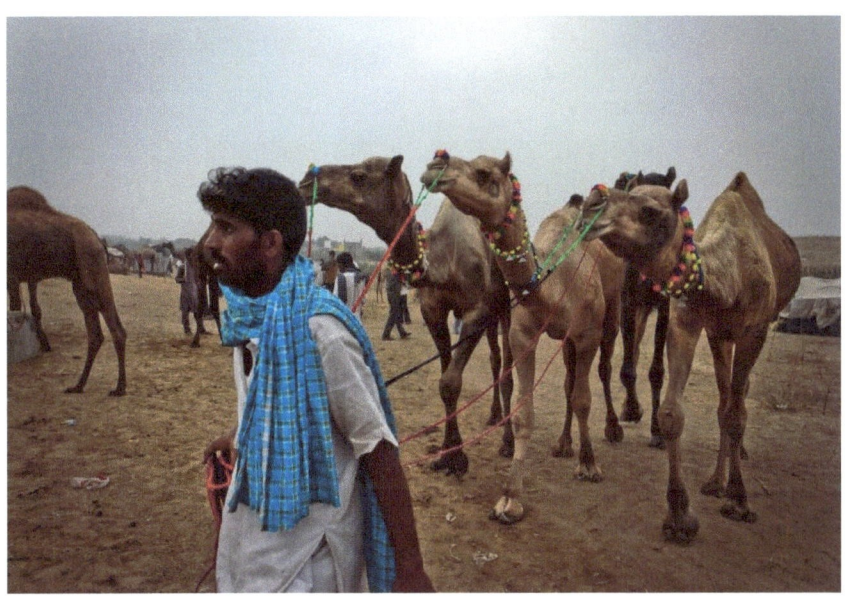

Camel sellers bringing the camels into the fair

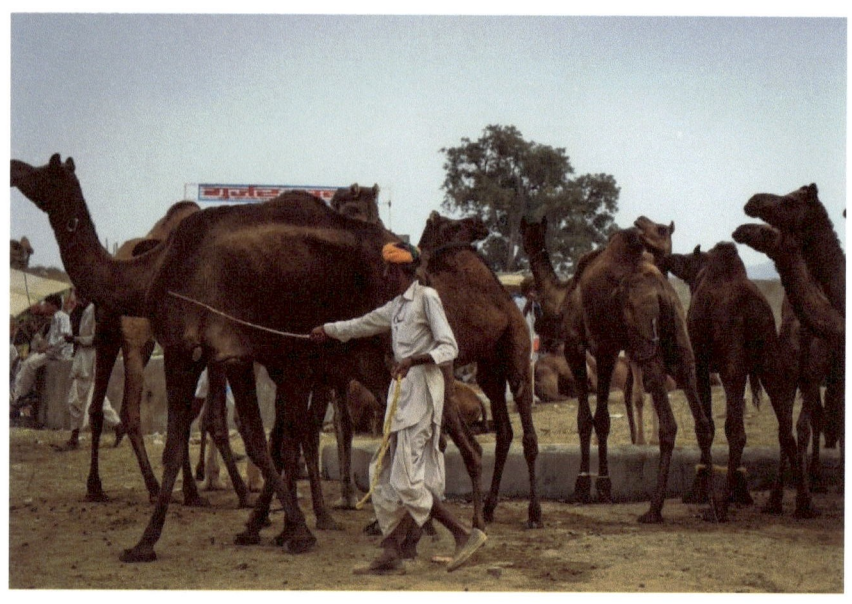

Stick for the rowdy ones

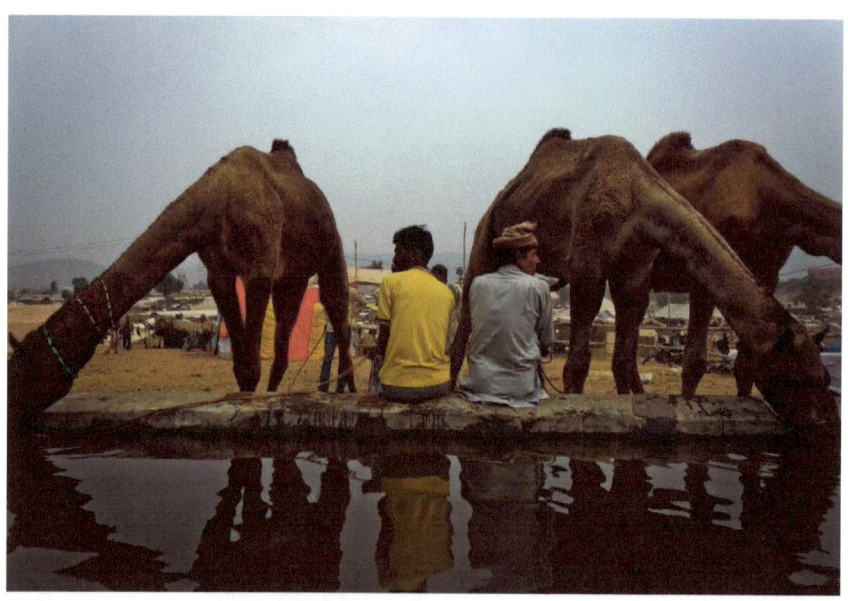

Camel wells built all over the place to feed the ships of desert

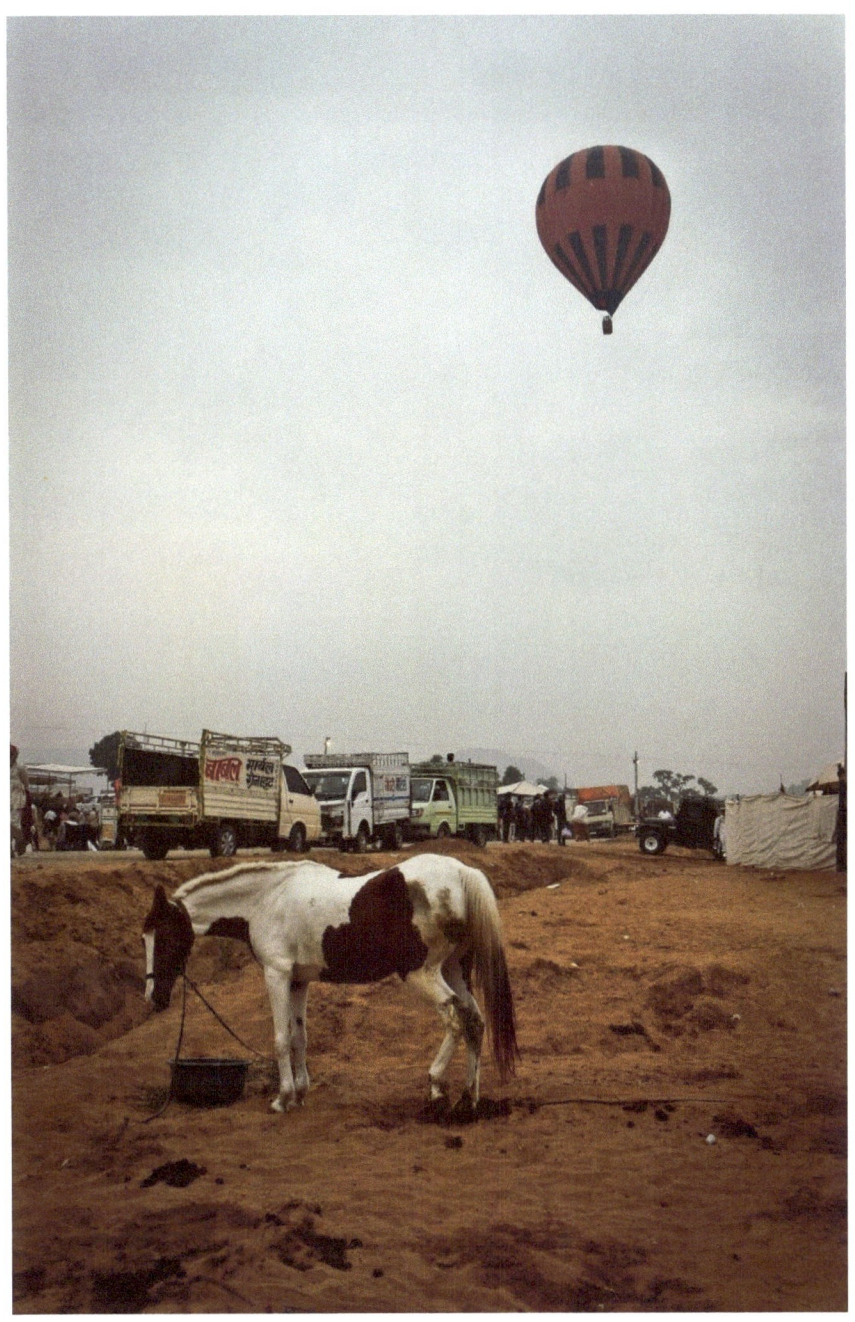

Hot air balloon takes its early morning flight over the marketplace

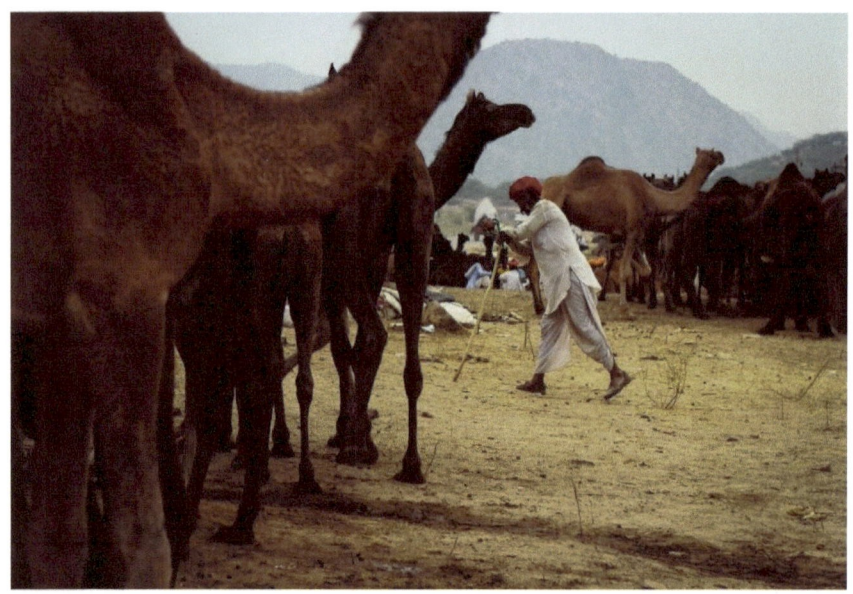

A seller keeping a watch on his camels

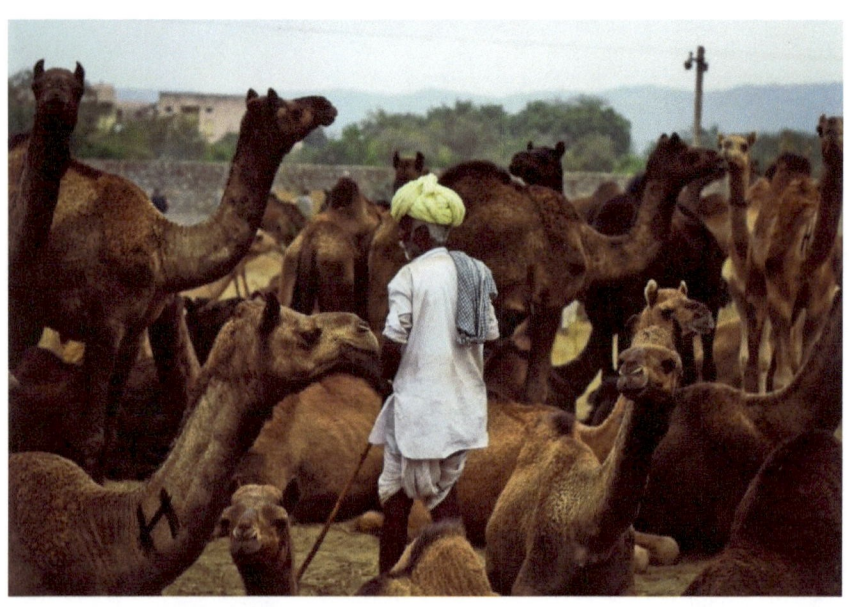

Another seller right into the middle of the group

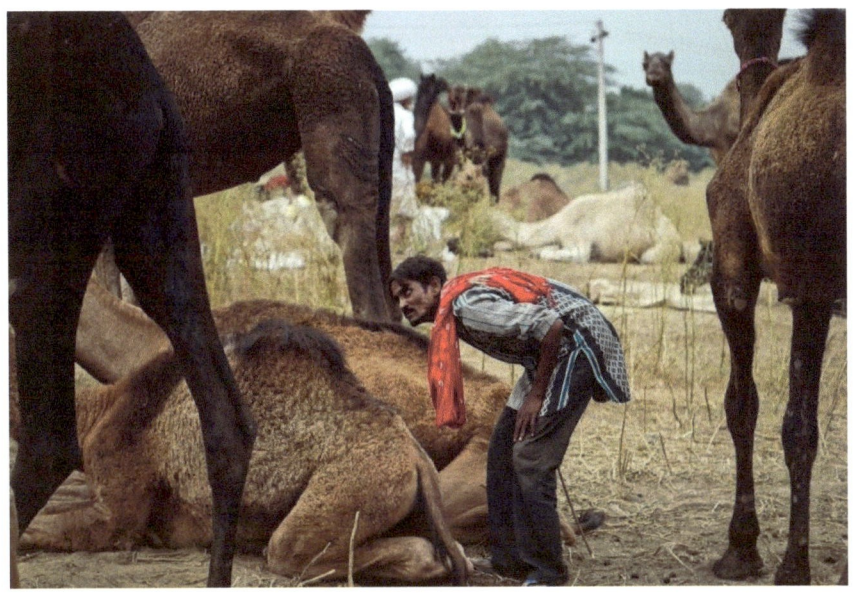

Not sure what inspection is being done here!

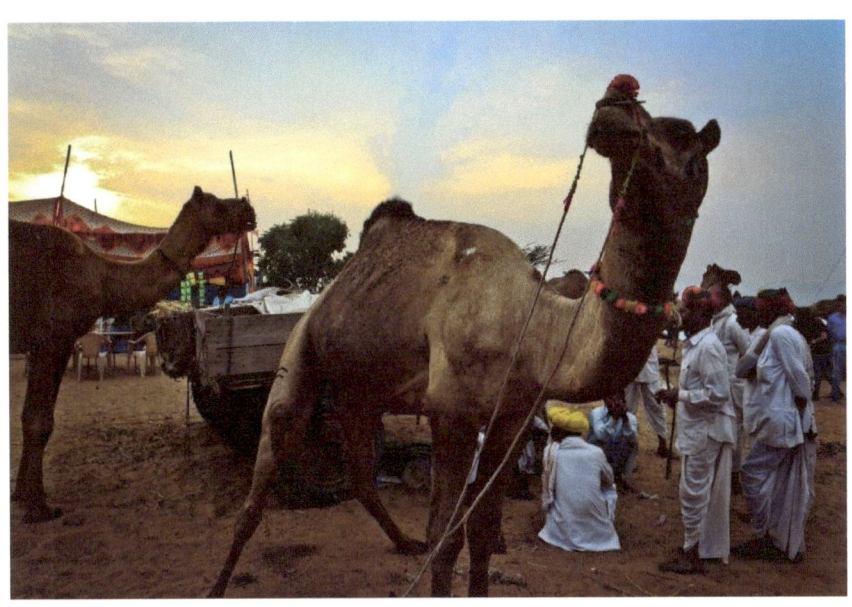

Here's a conversation happening between the sellers as the day draws to its end

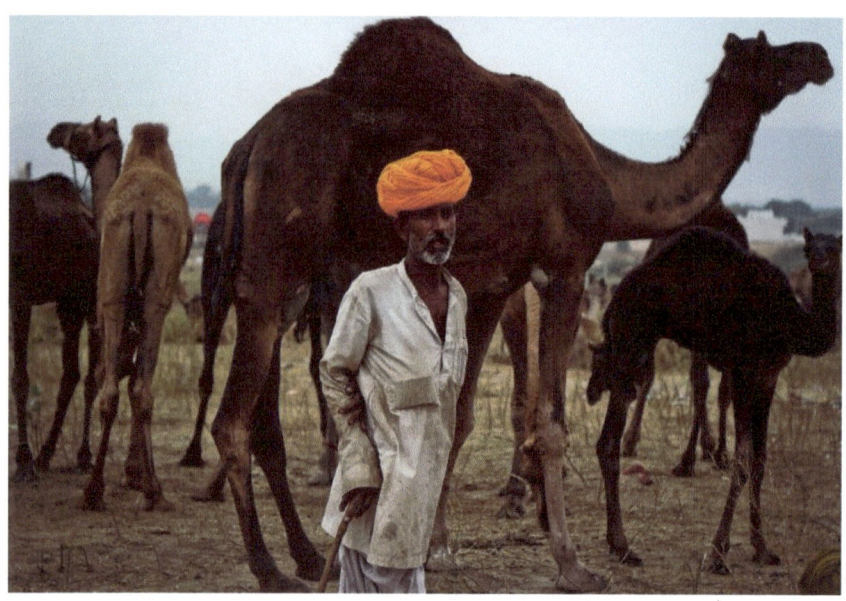

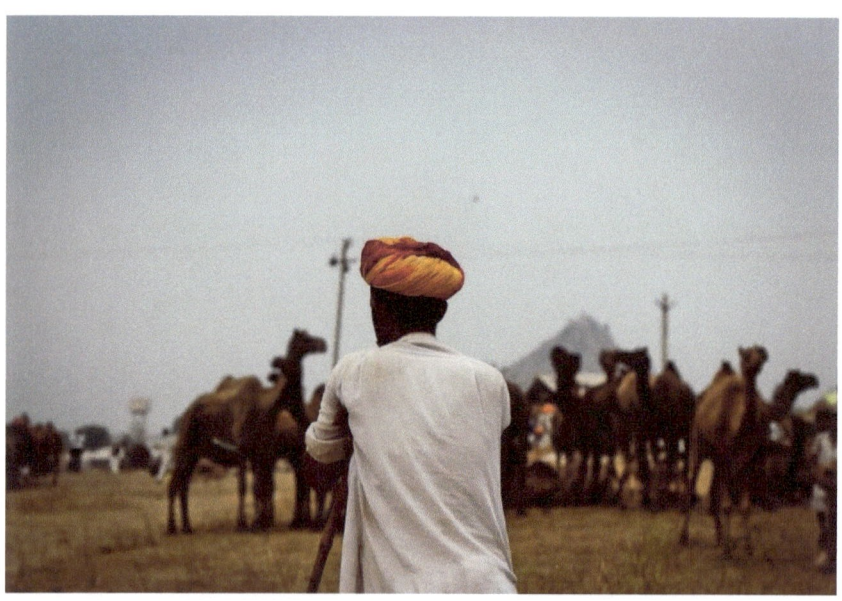

With those colorful turbans up on their head the sellers hold the ground for all five days

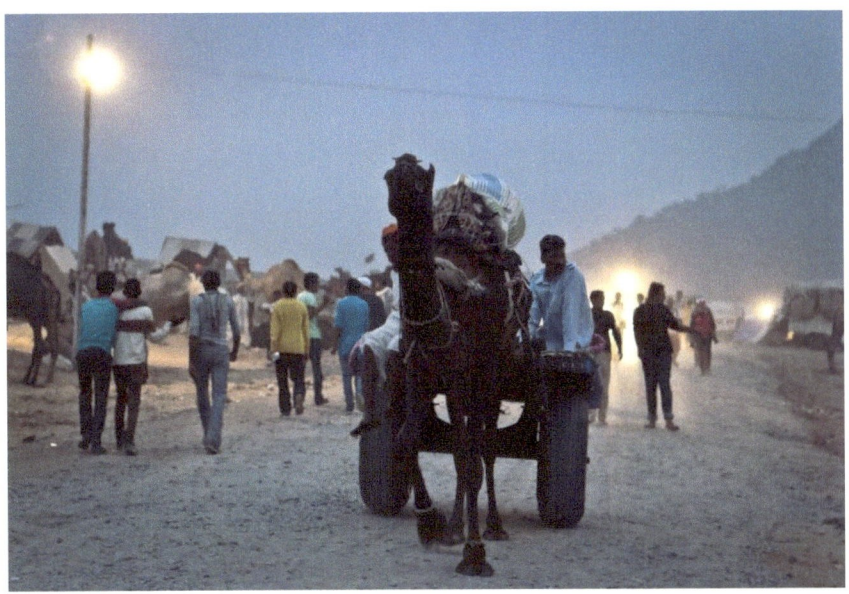

As the sun begins to set the entire areas becomes so mesmerizing you can't take your eyes off it

2. UP CLOSE

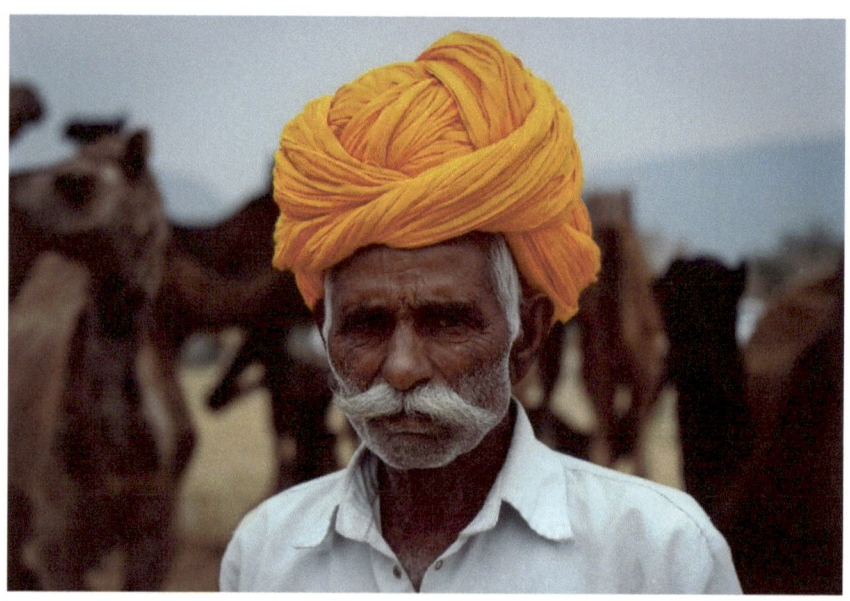

A regular seller at the fair since last 20 years

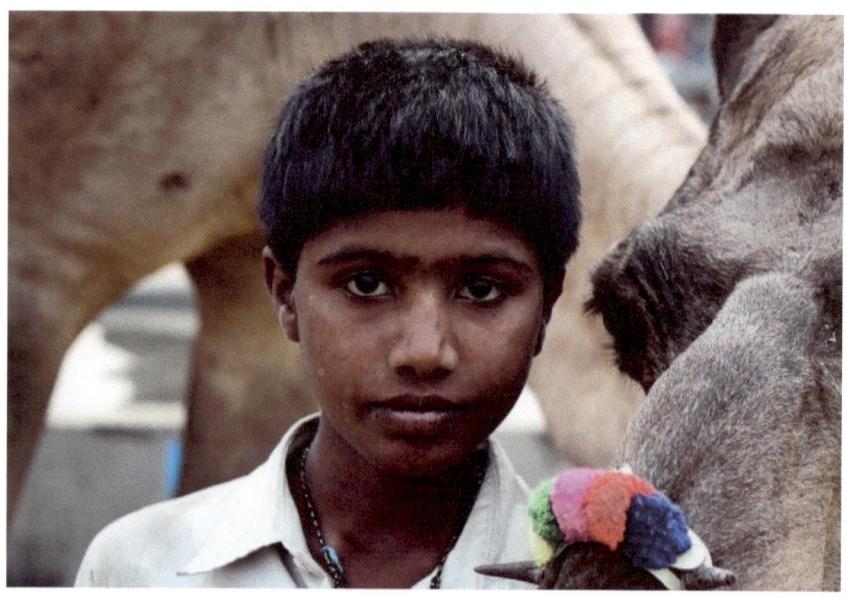

A young boy who was eager to be clicked

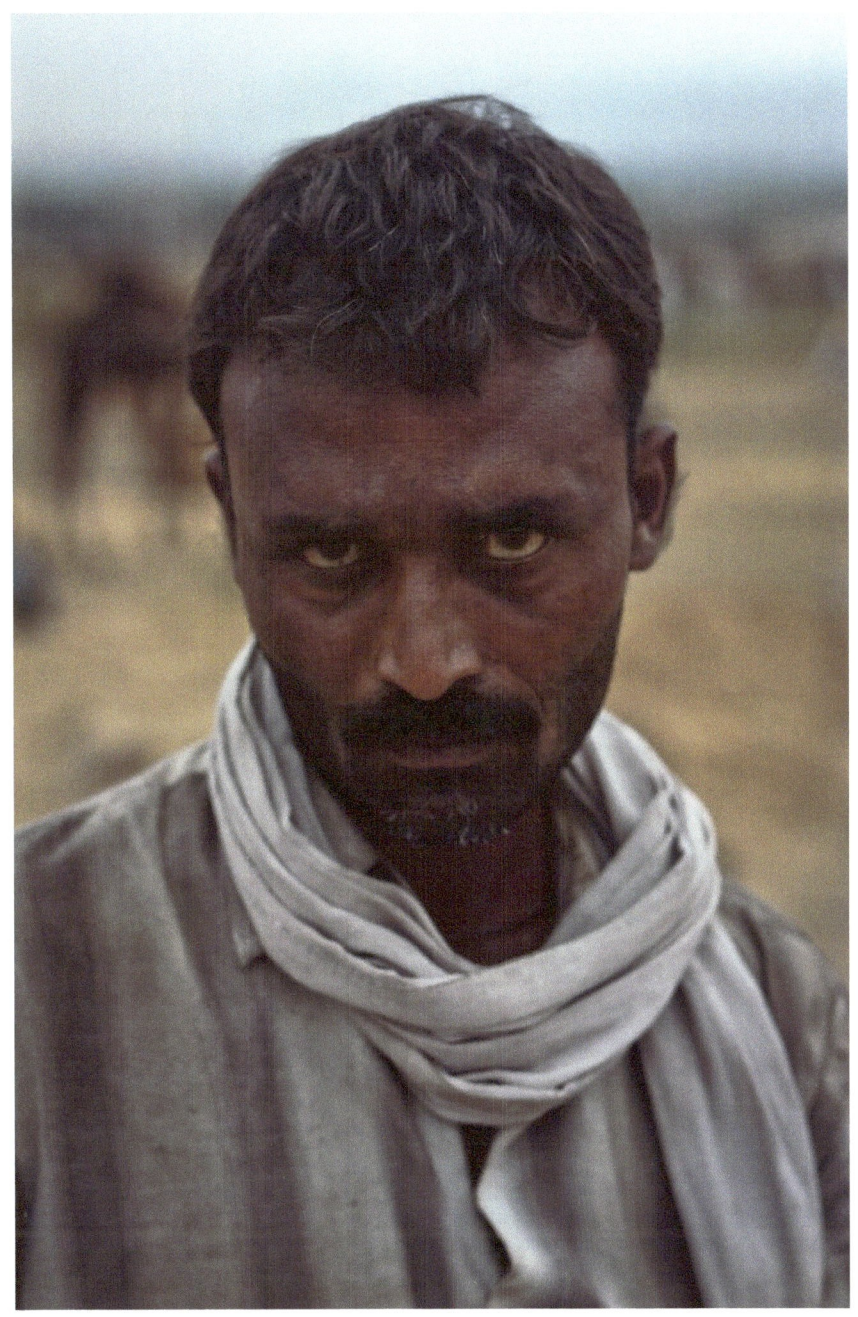

An instrument player who plays the traditional sarangi to earn his livelihood

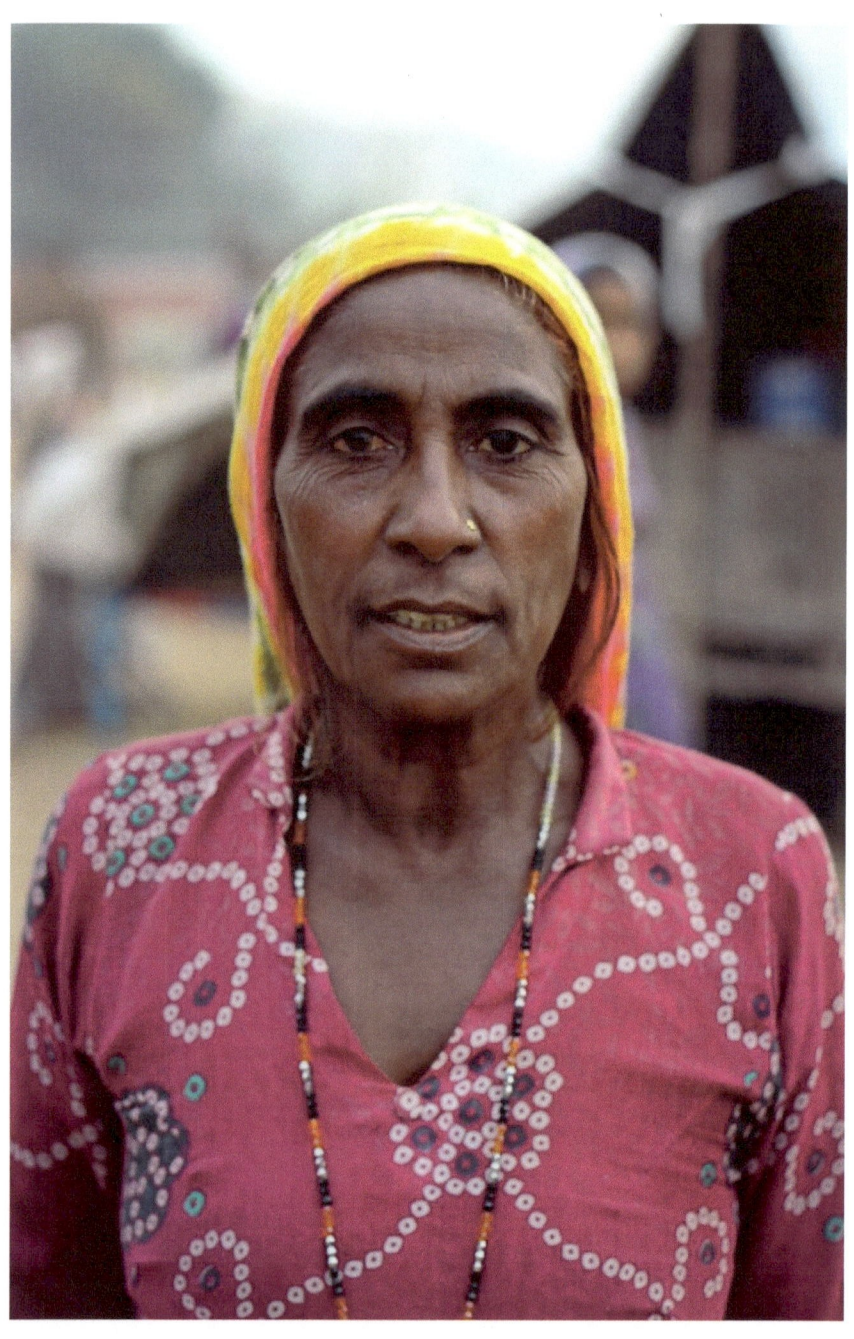

Portrait of a traditional women

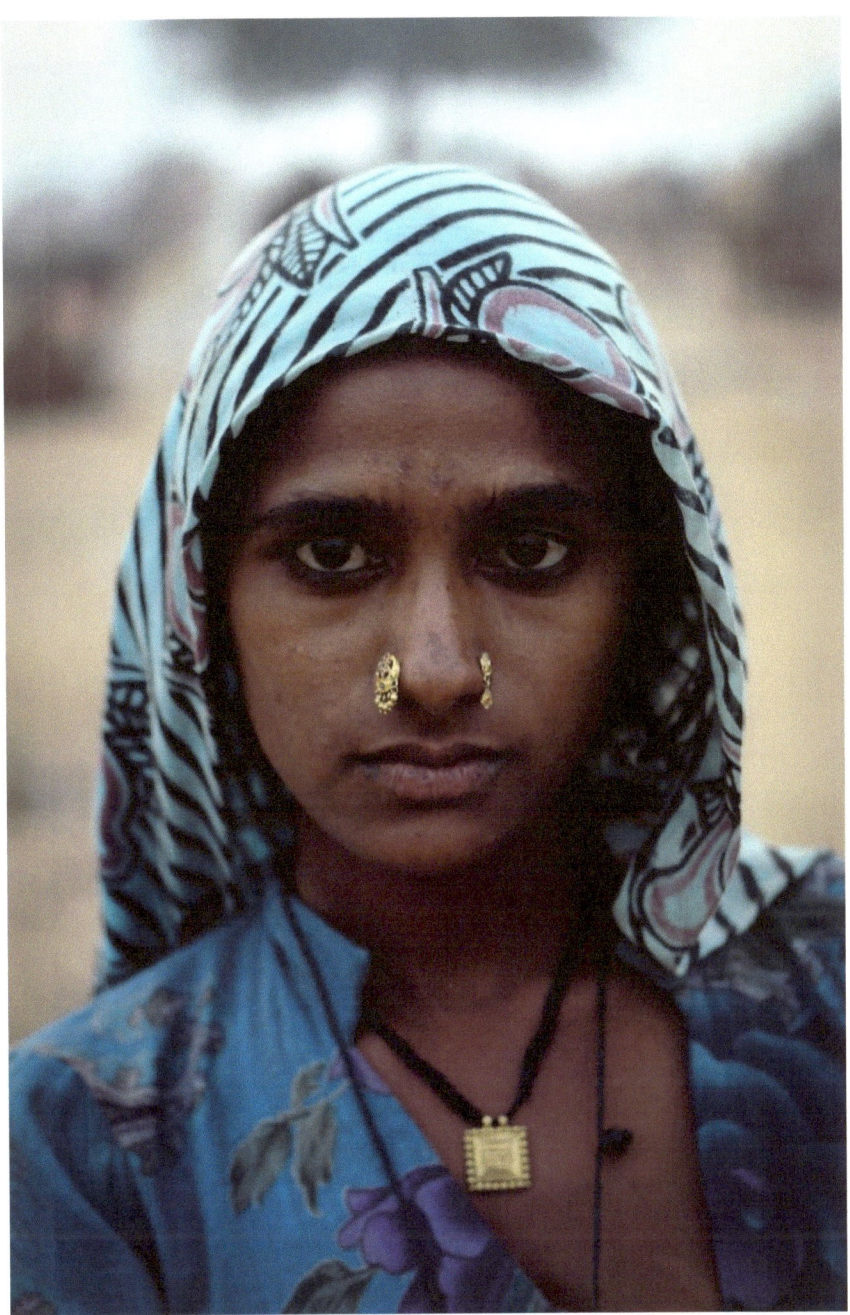

Portrait of a traditional women

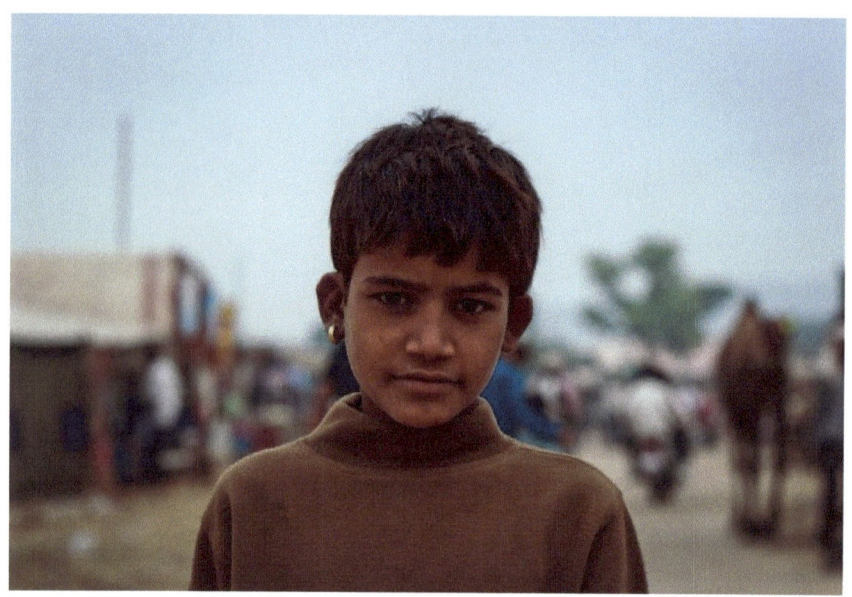

Young soul who was very glad to see his picture on the camera screen

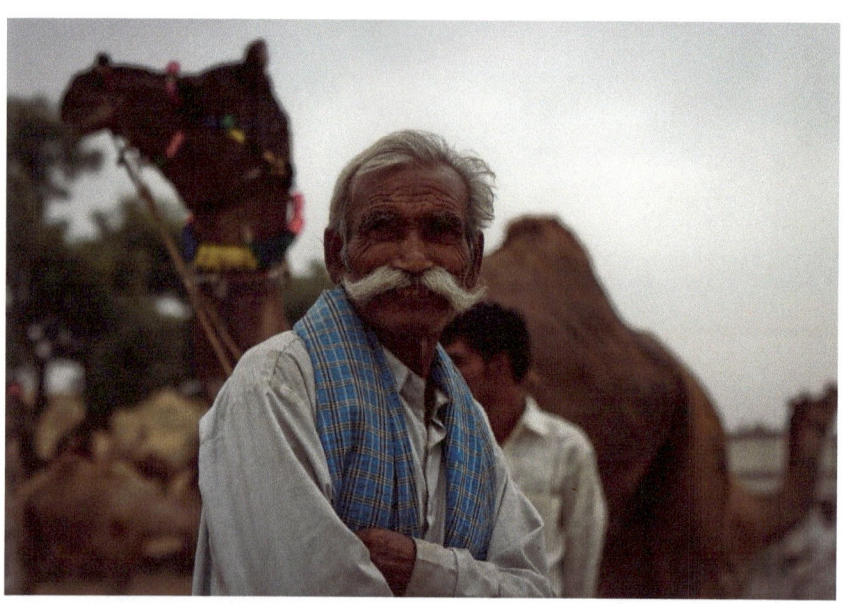

Those moustaches!

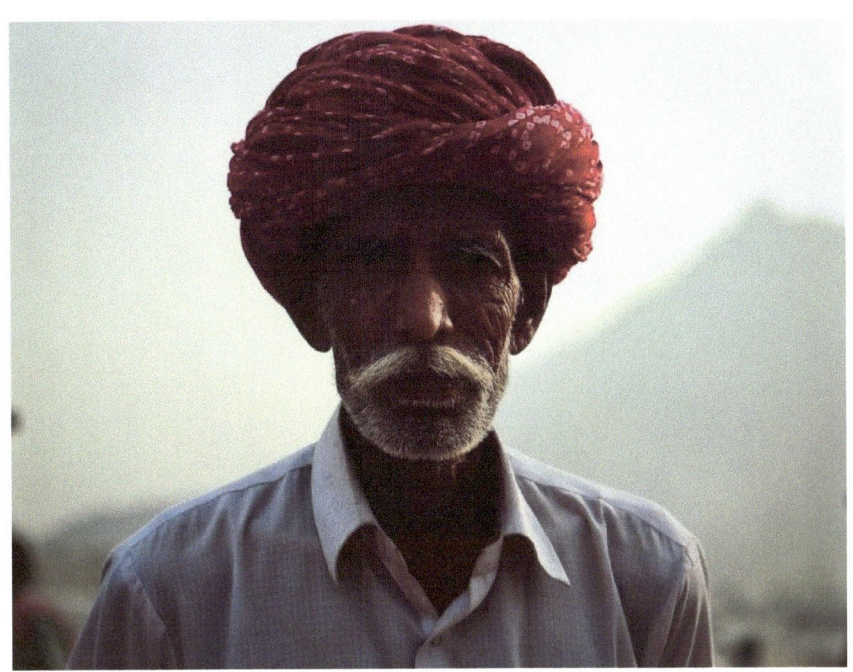

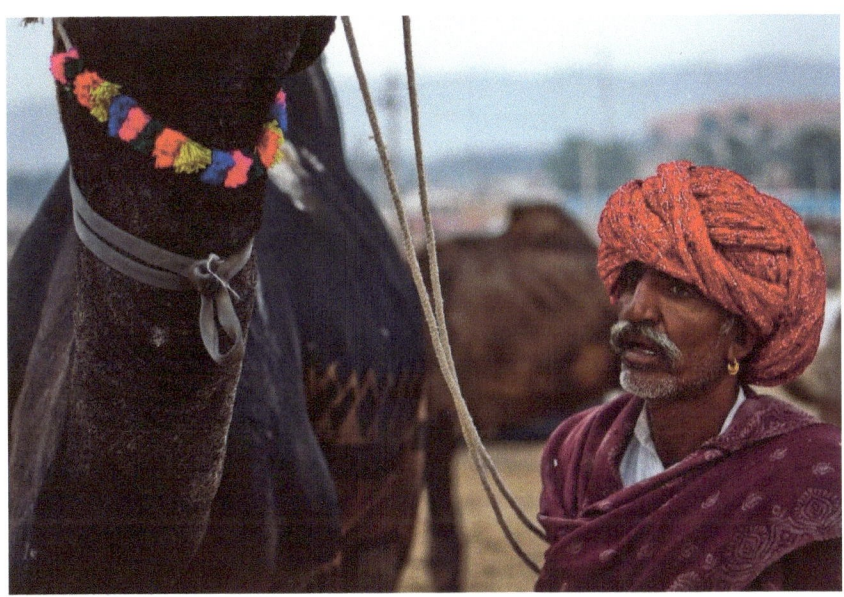

The colorful turbans are a common sight across the fair

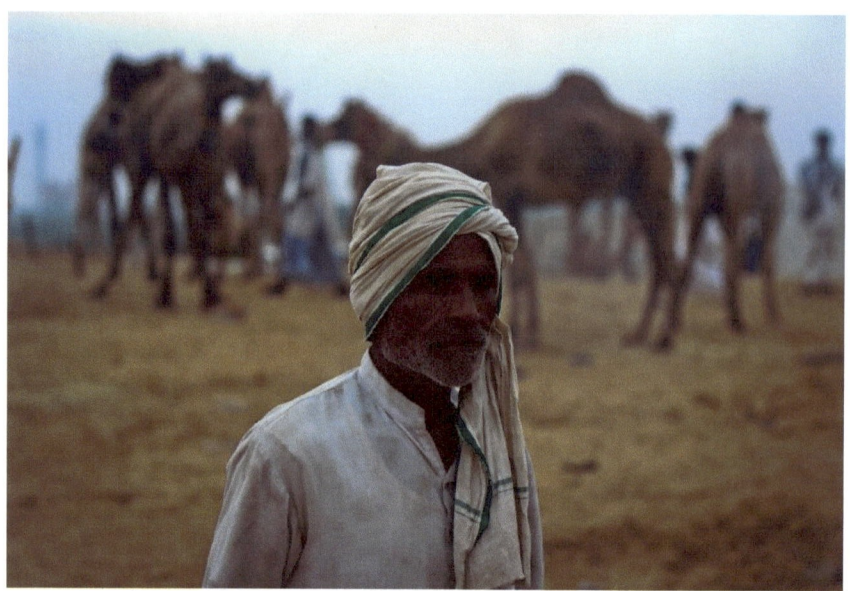

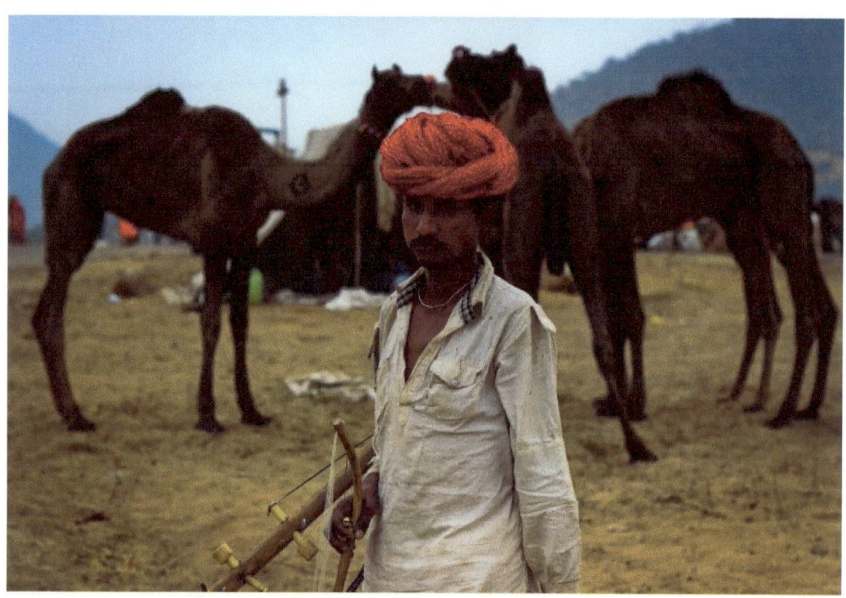

To each his own thoughts!

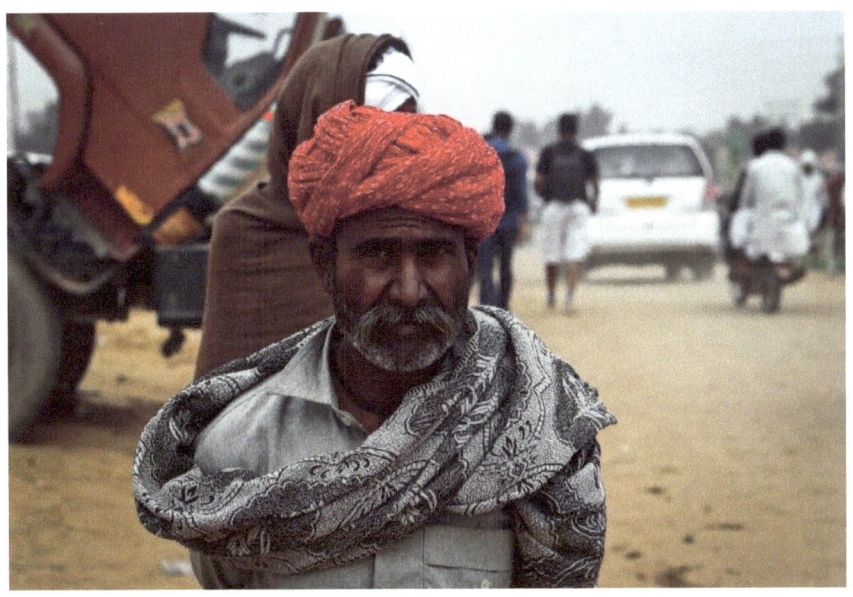

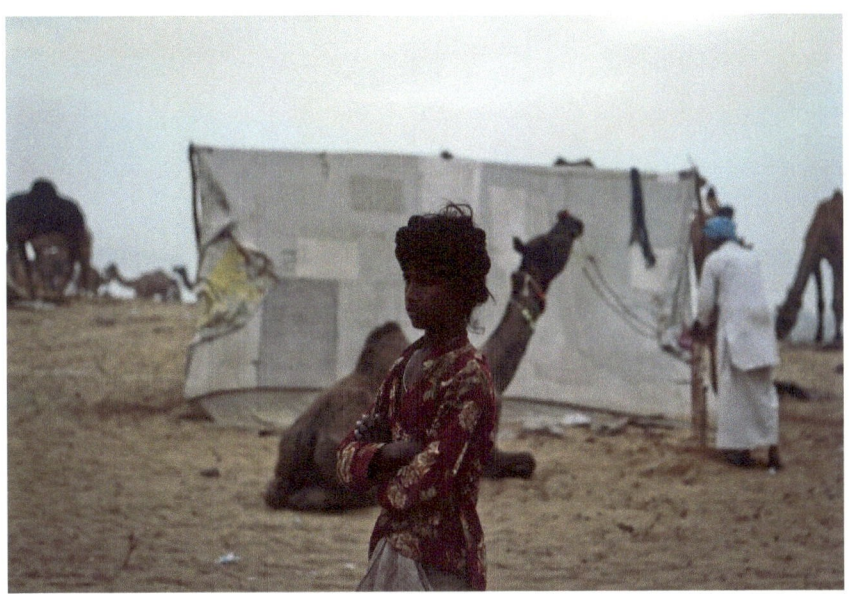

To each his own thoughts!

3. THE YOUNG SOULS

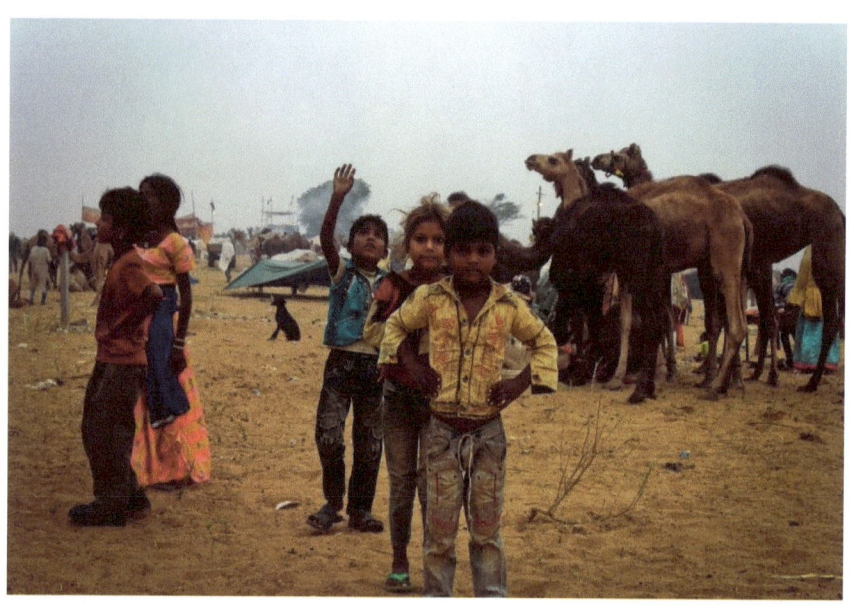

Some kids eager to get clicked while the others in total awe of the flying hot air balloon

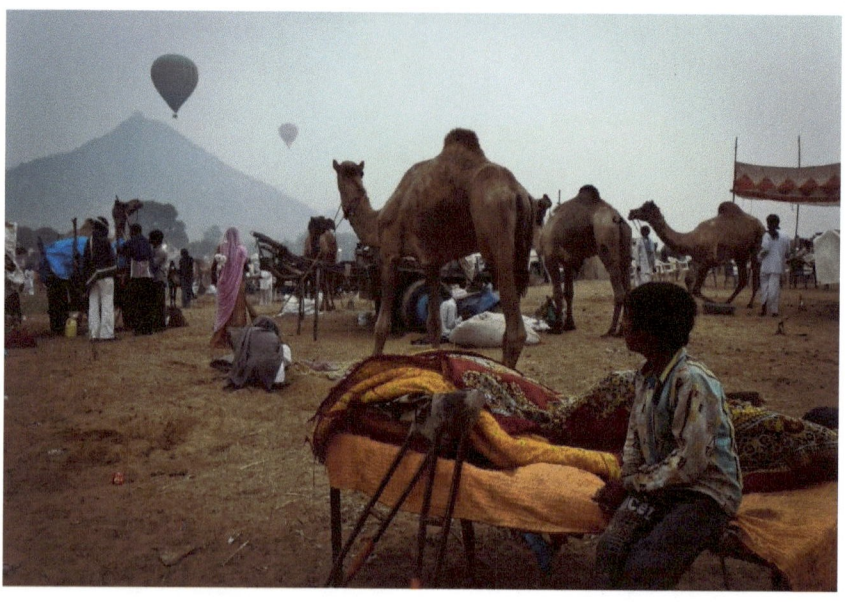

The hot air balloons seemed to be the candy of everyone's eye at the fair

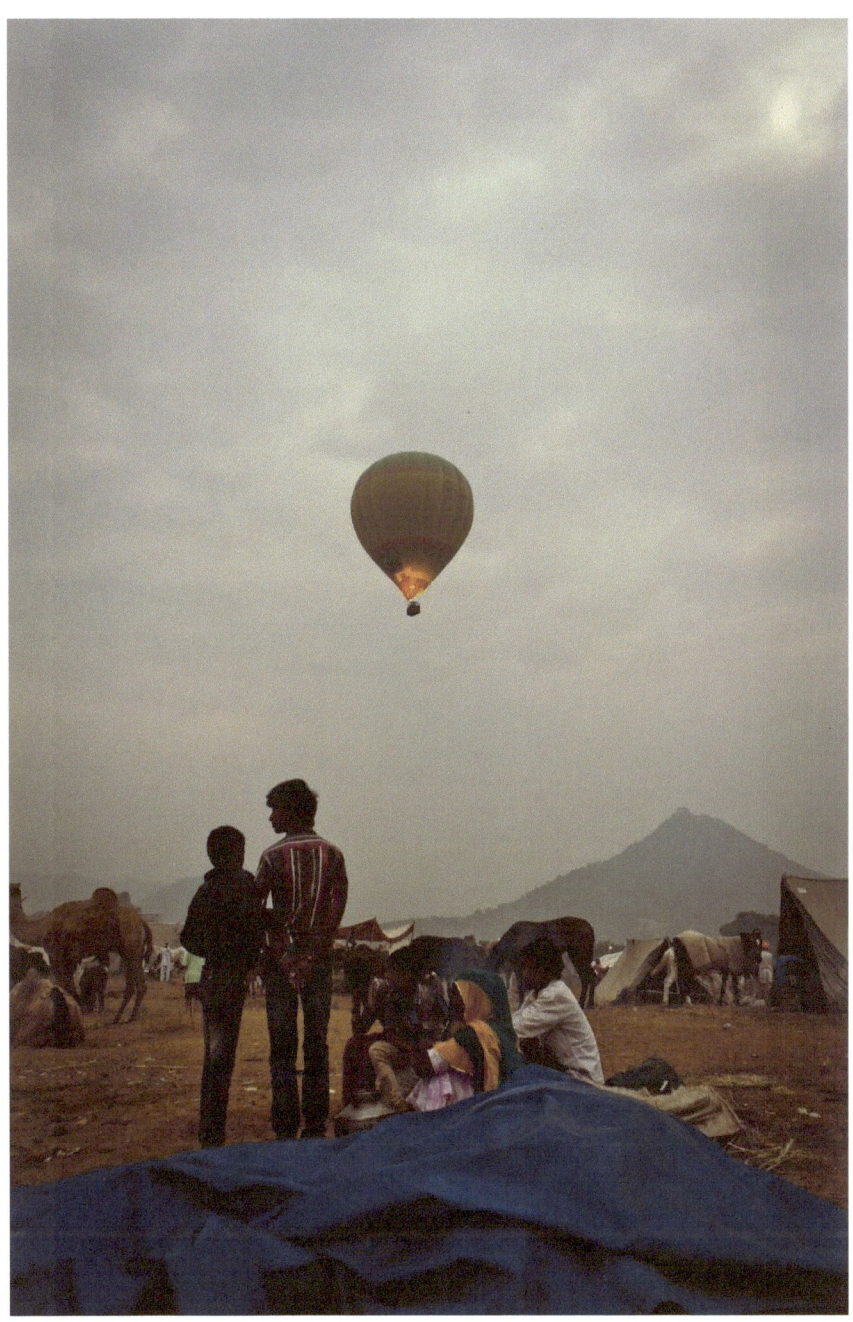

The hot air balloons seemed to be the candy of everyone's eye at the fair

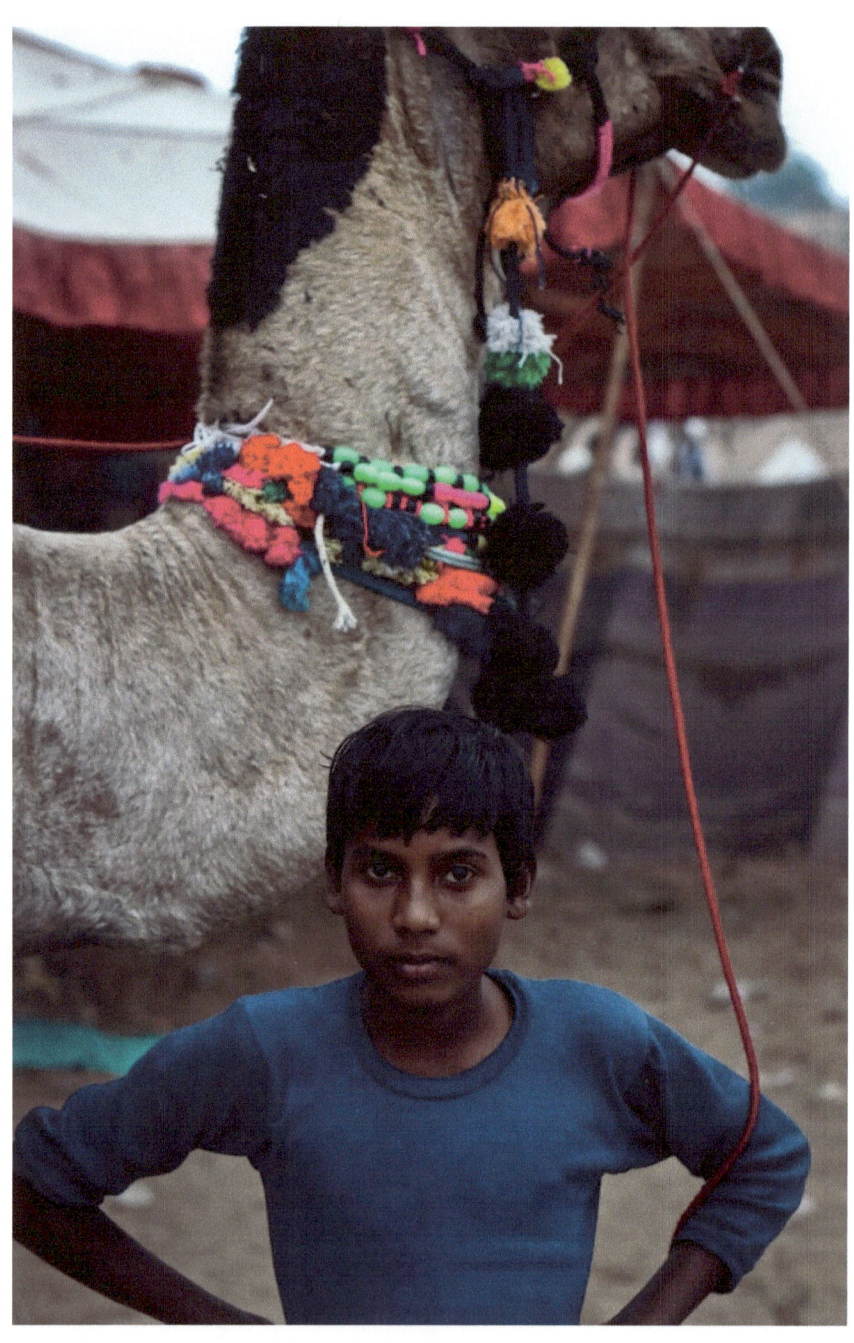

Perhaps the young lad's first selling junket to the Pushkar Fair

20

4. CONVERSATIONS

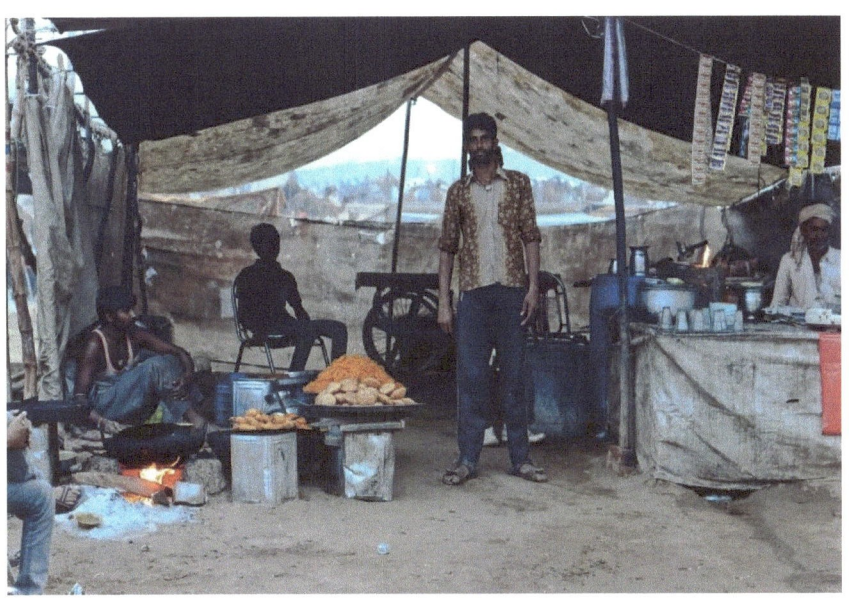

Roadside dhaba serving food and local delicacies to the visitors

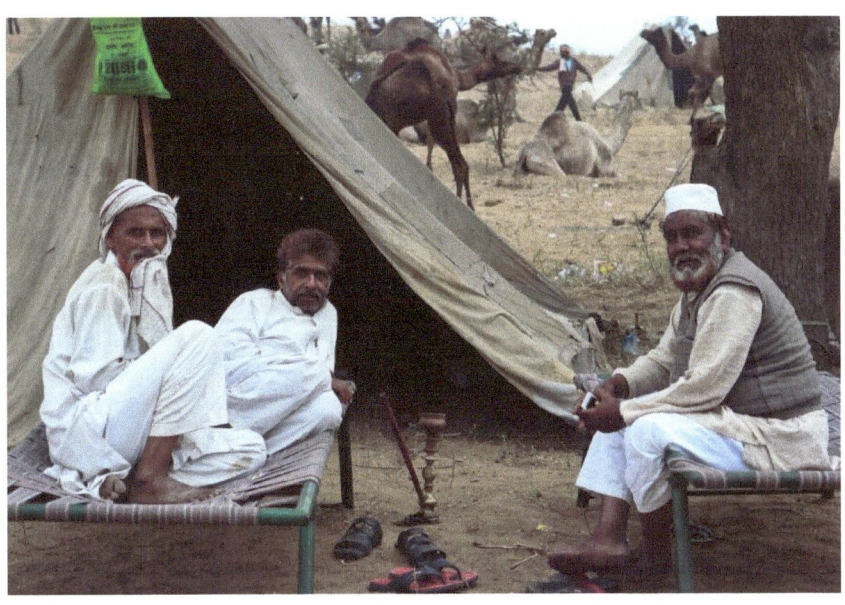

Elderly men engaged in a serious discussion were very happy to get clicked

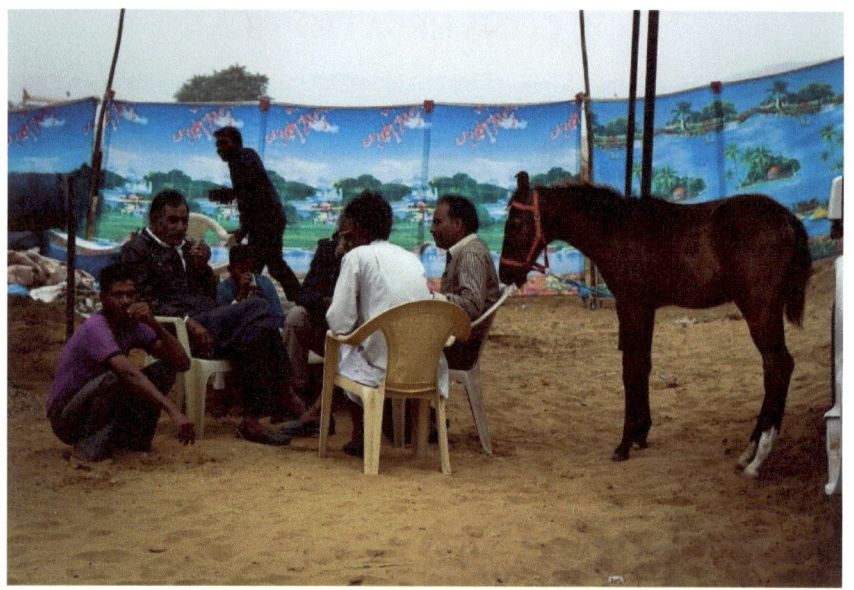

And, the discussions continue unabated throughout the day

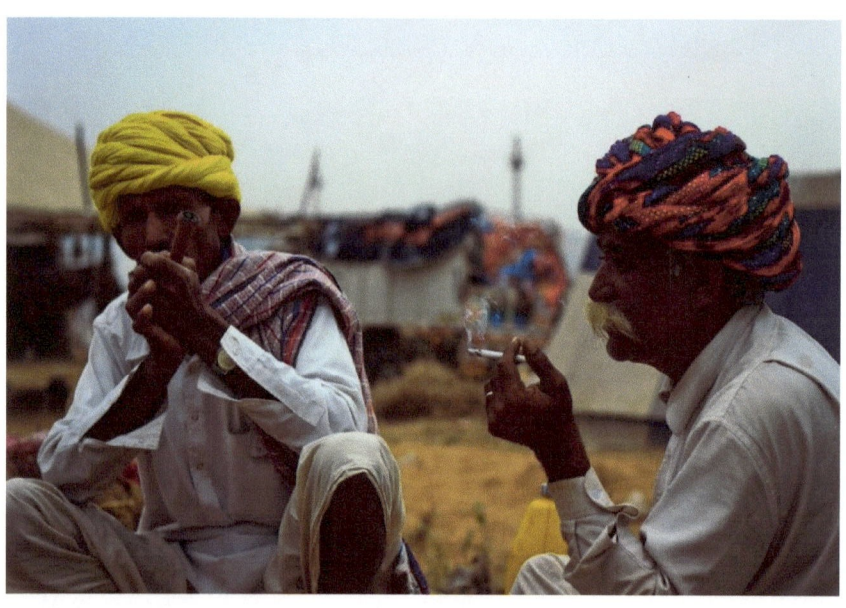

The chillums comes as a welcome respite to the heavy lifting done throughout the day for these elderly men

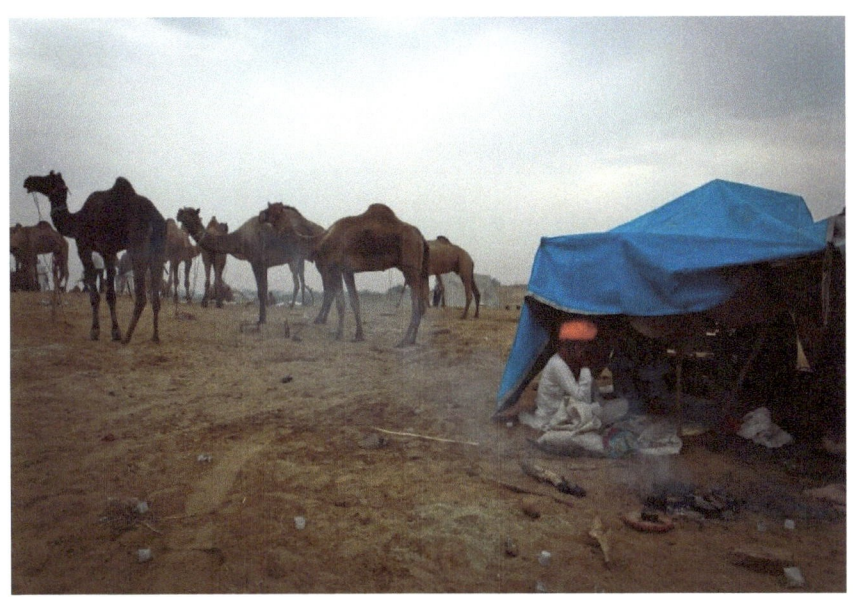

An early morning phone conversation

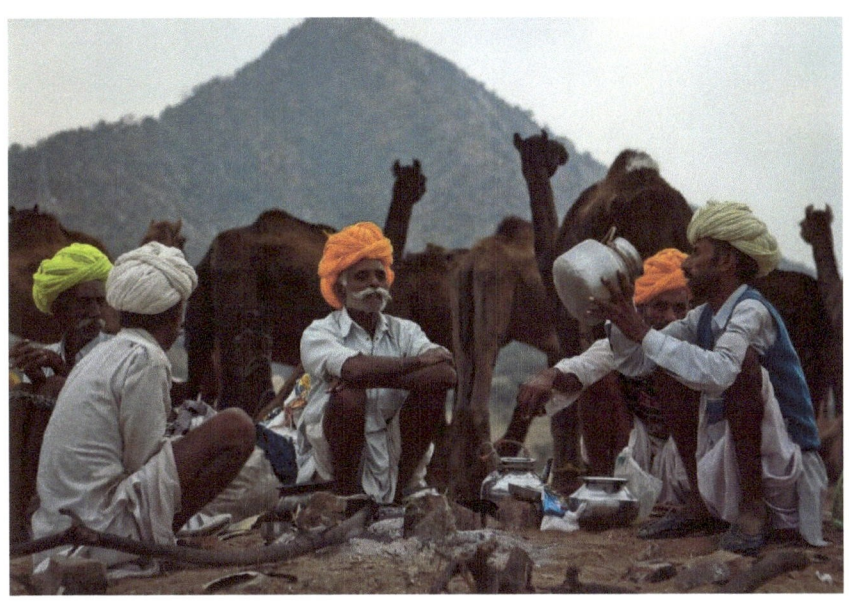

A late evening conversation

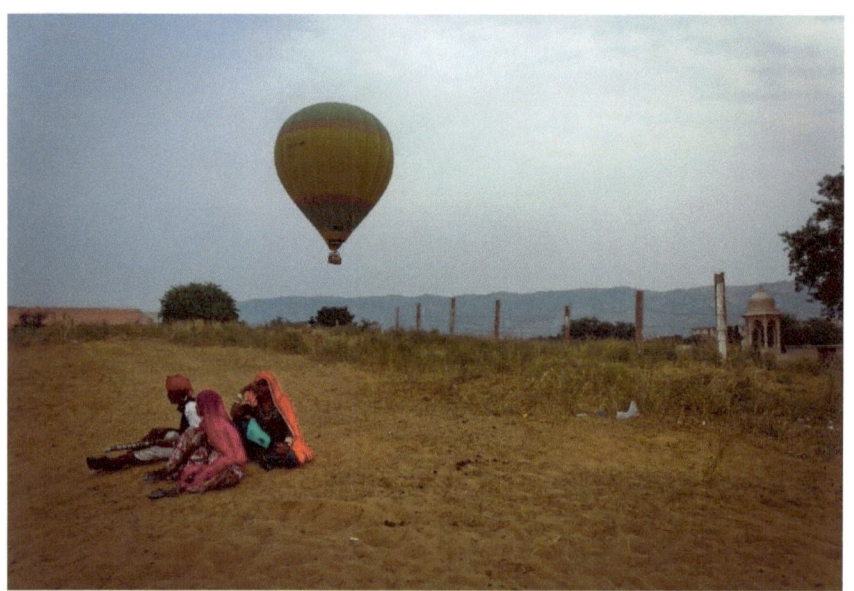

A family reciting traditional songs as the hot air balloon takes it last flight for the day

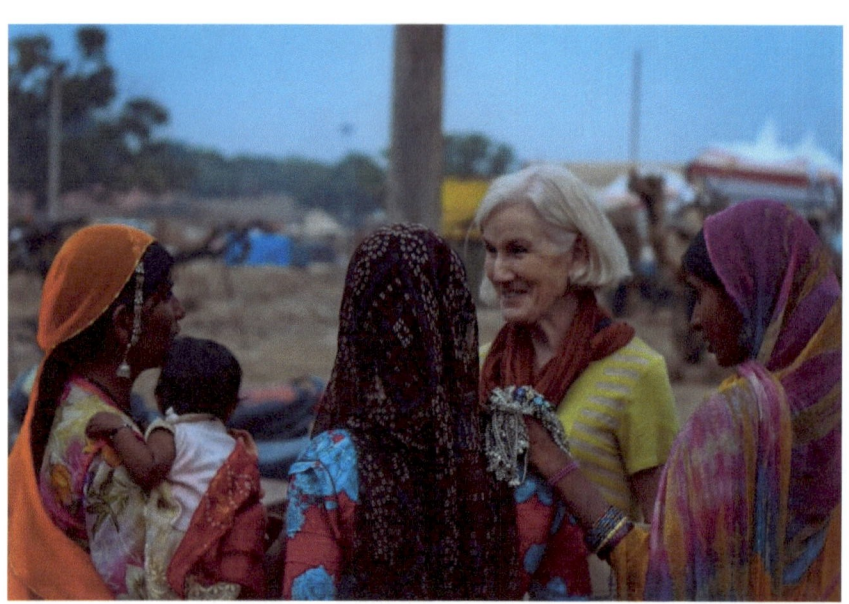

Women banter

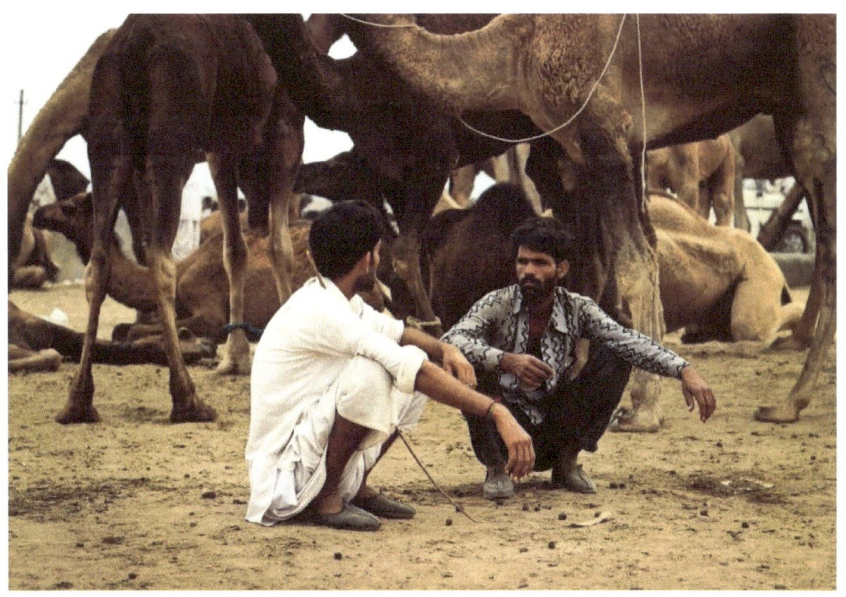

How many did you manage to sell, eh?

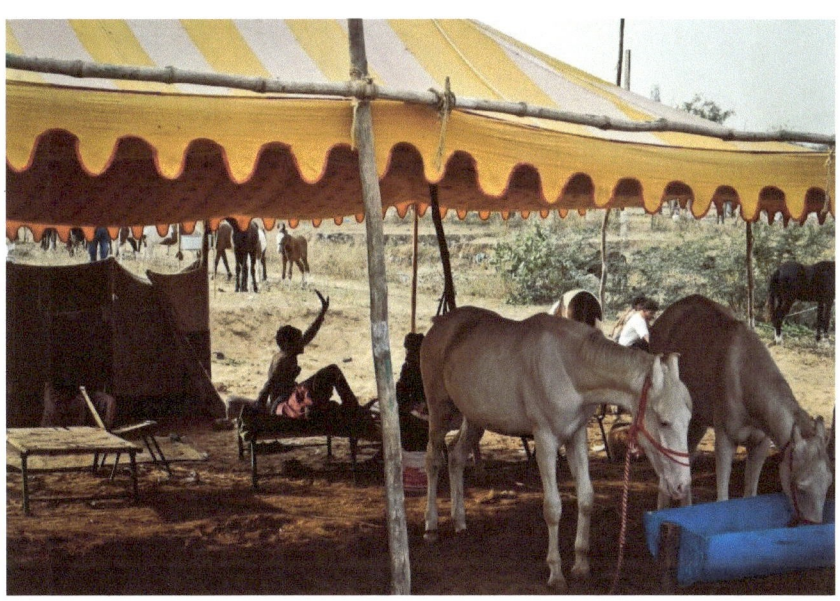

Everyone has a story to tell, here!

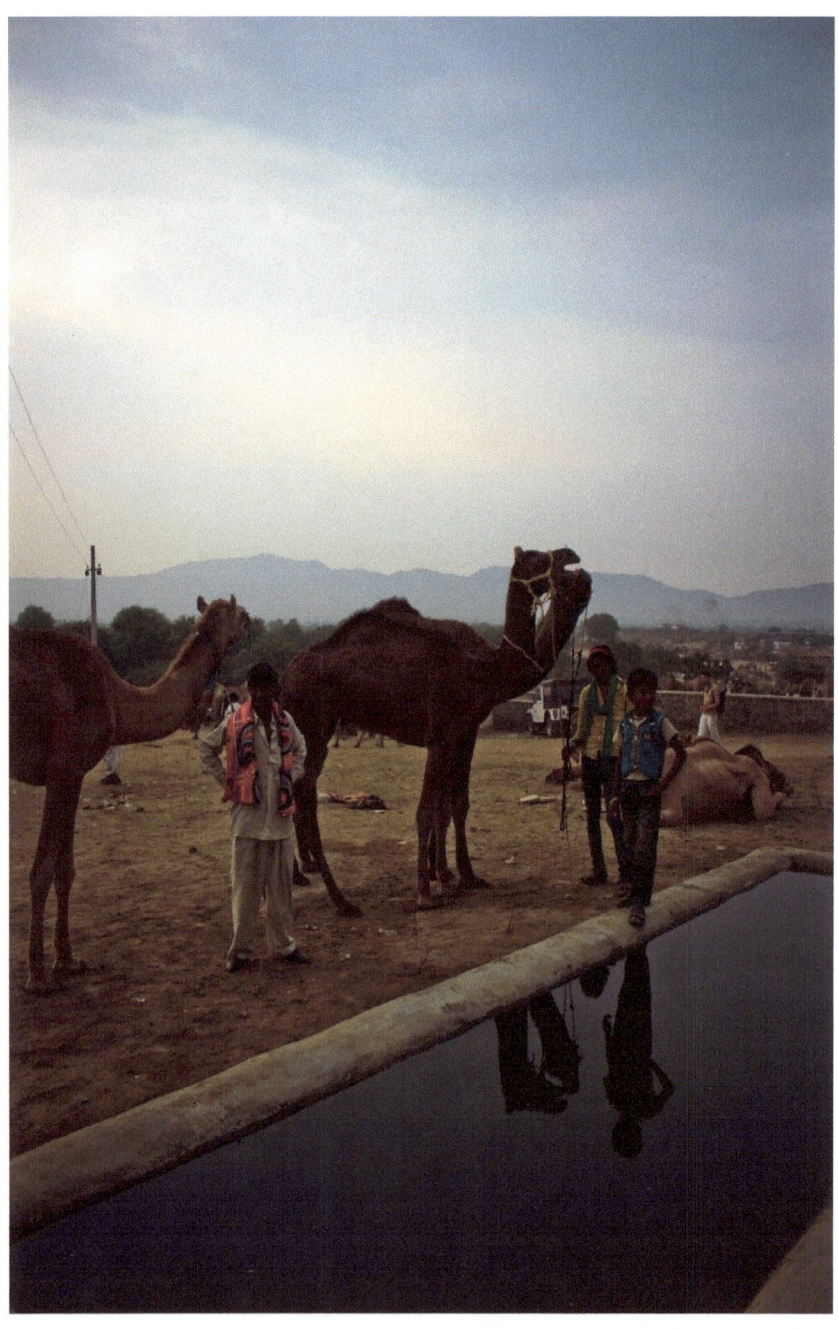

Camel pond to feed them

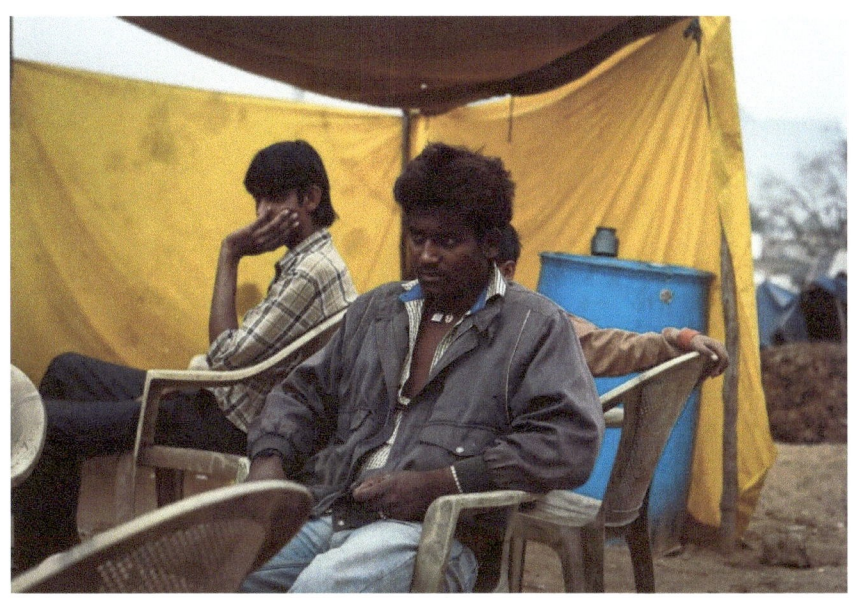

Why so serious?

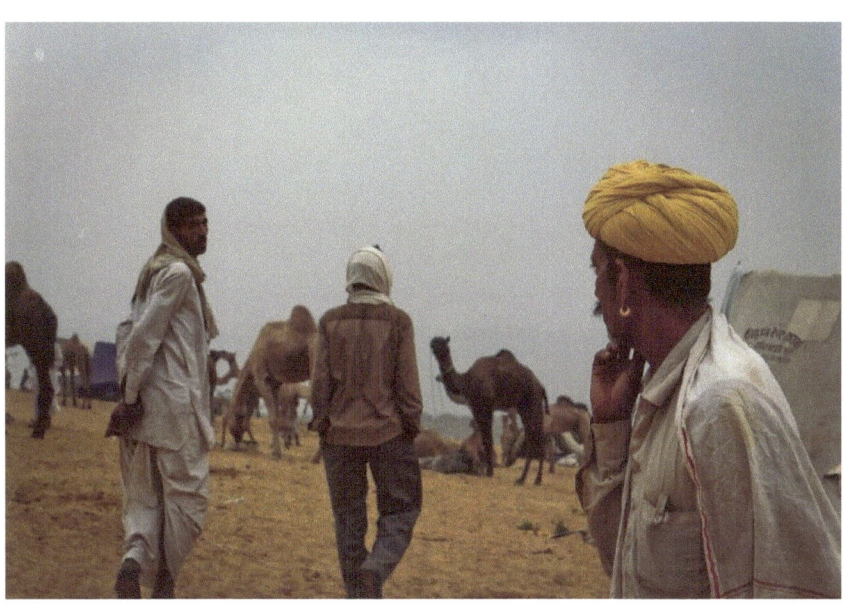

The last minute reminder

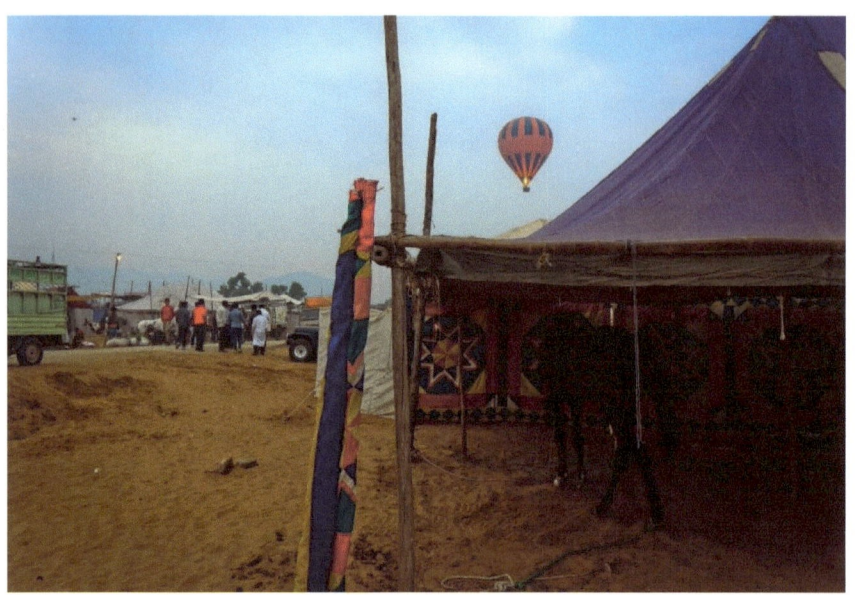

The lone horse!

5. AT WORK

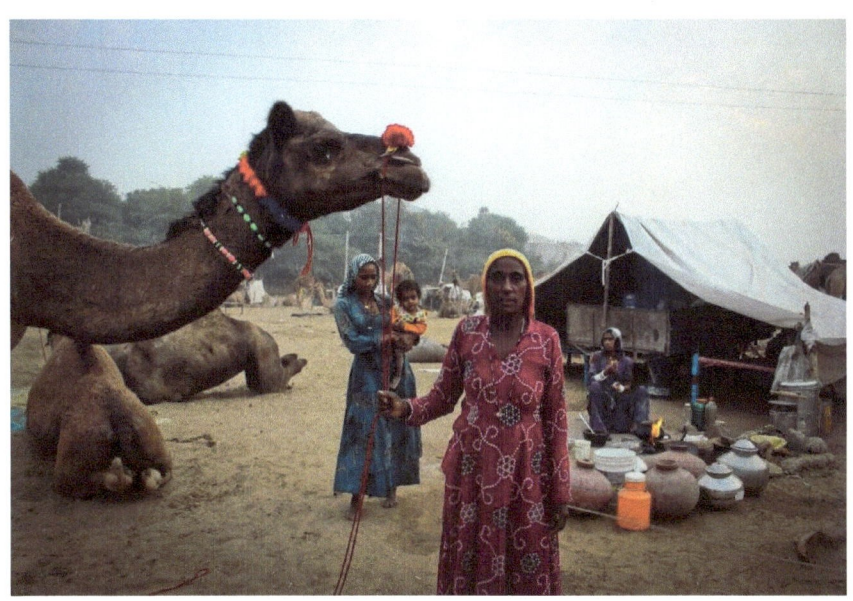

In front of their tent selling camels, as the dusk sets in

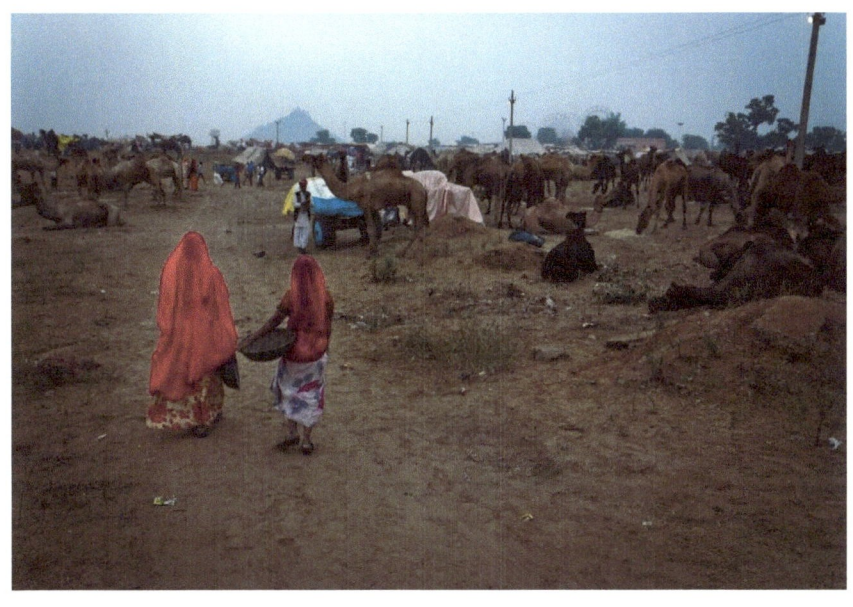

Mother and daughter

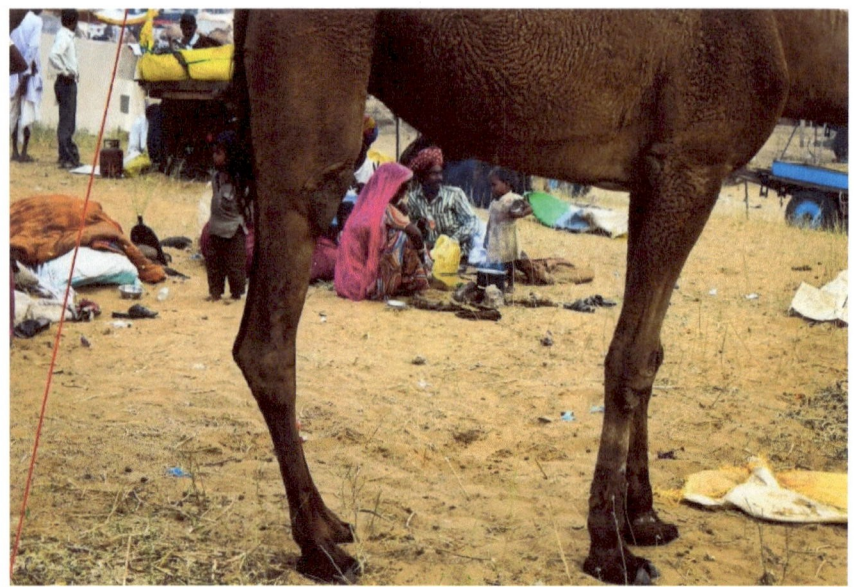

Lunch time!

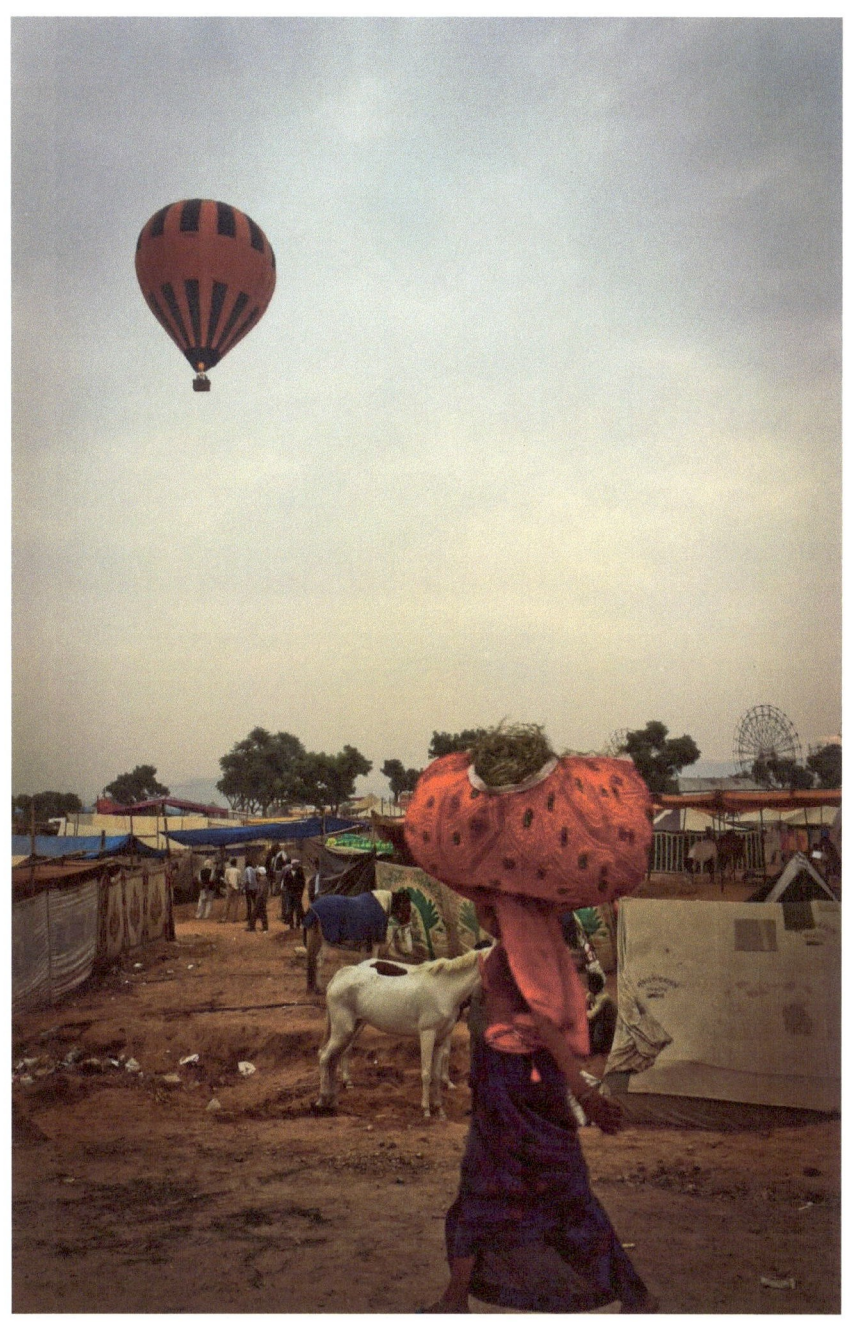

First morning flight

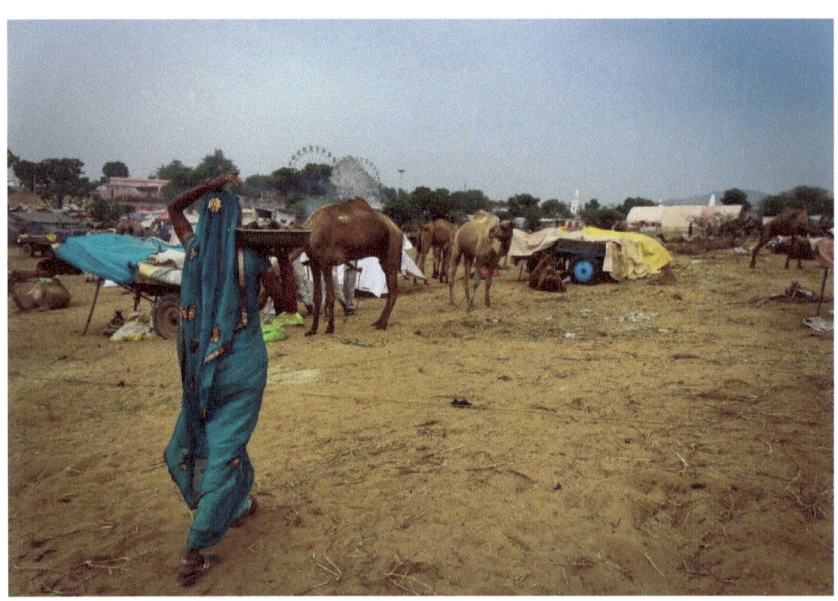

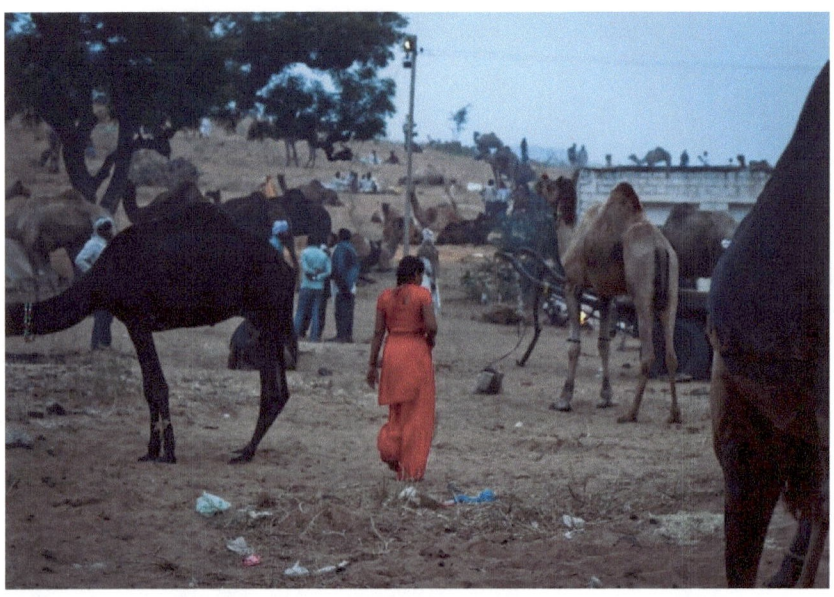

A woman carrying fodder for the cattle

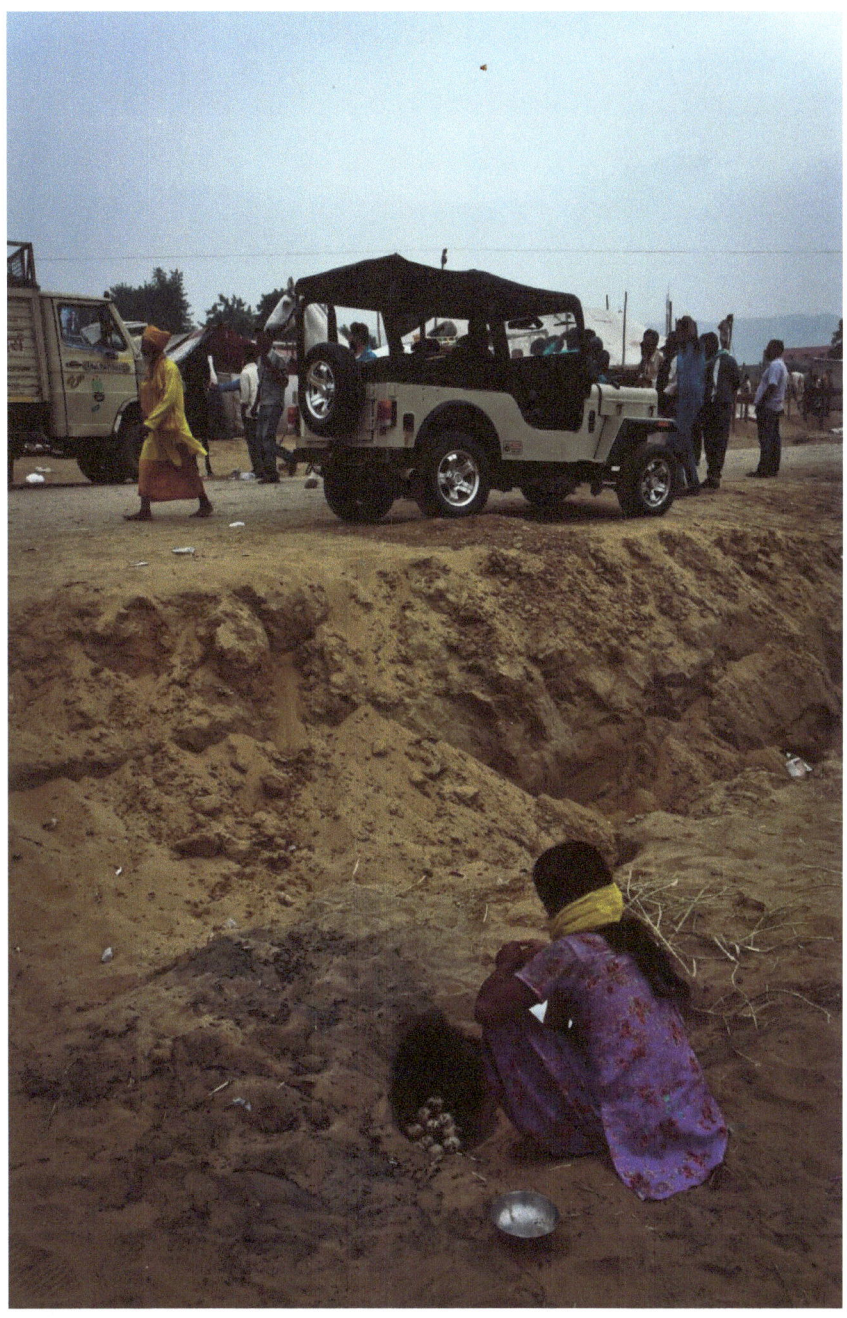

A woman cooking bhaati in a traditional furnace (tandoor)

6. CAVALCADES

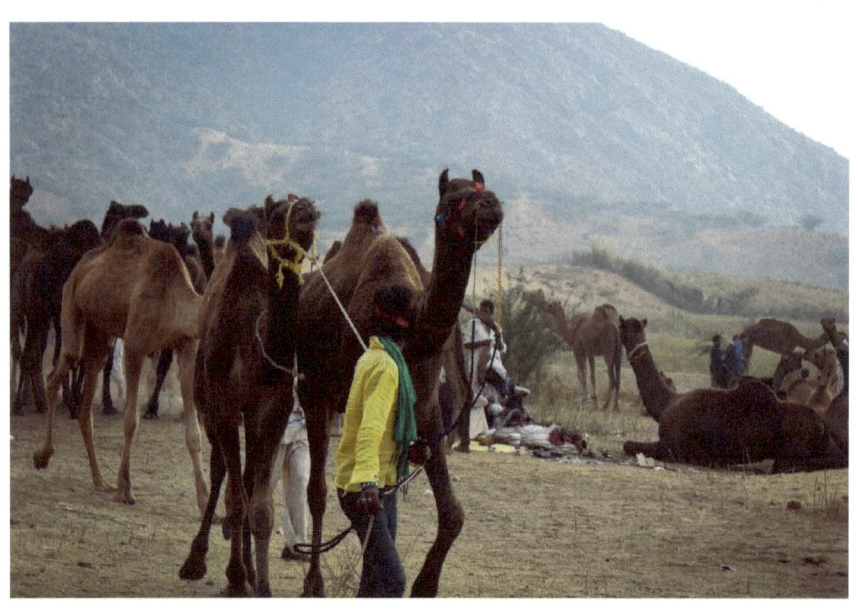

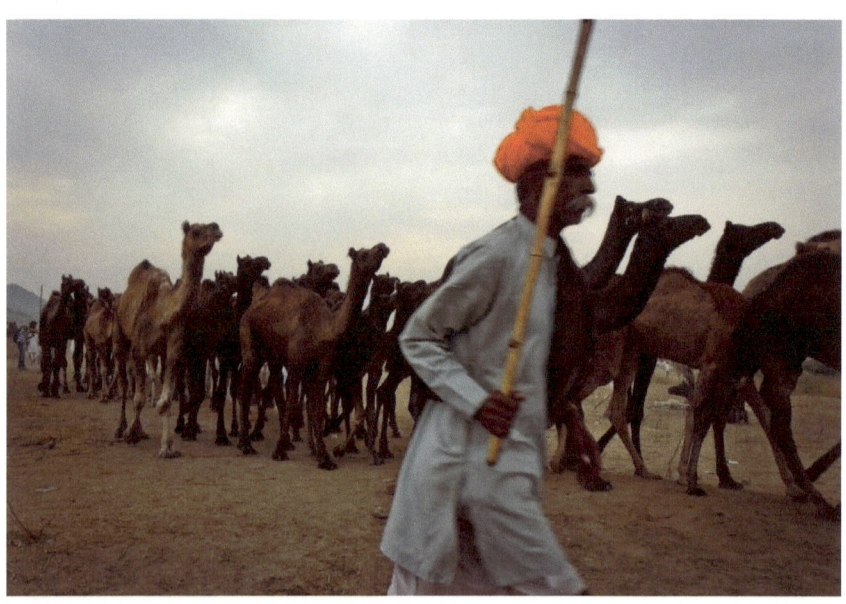

With their camels all over the place!

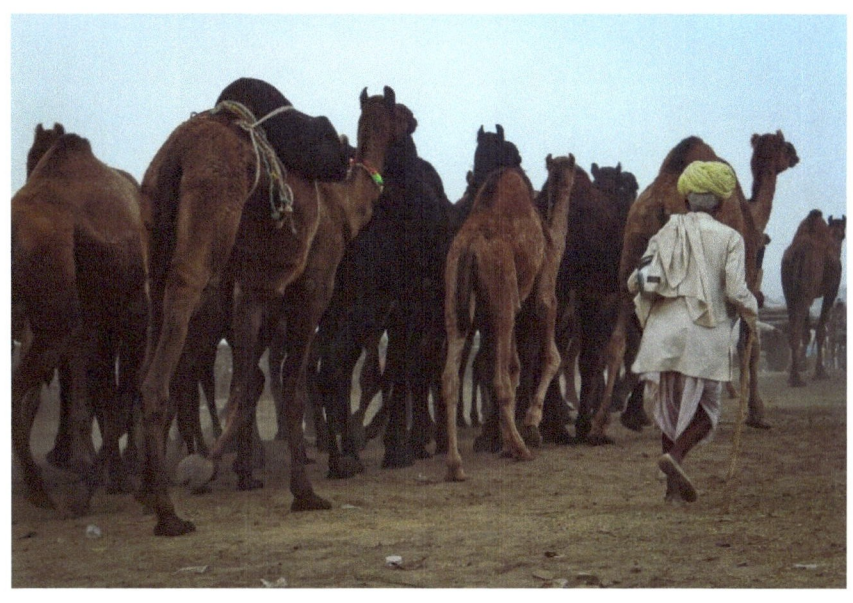

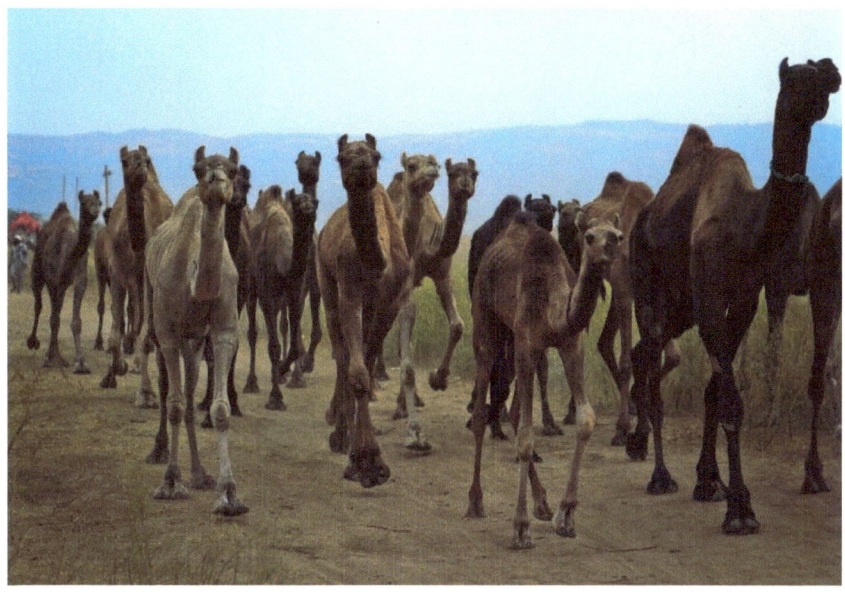

With their camels all over the place!

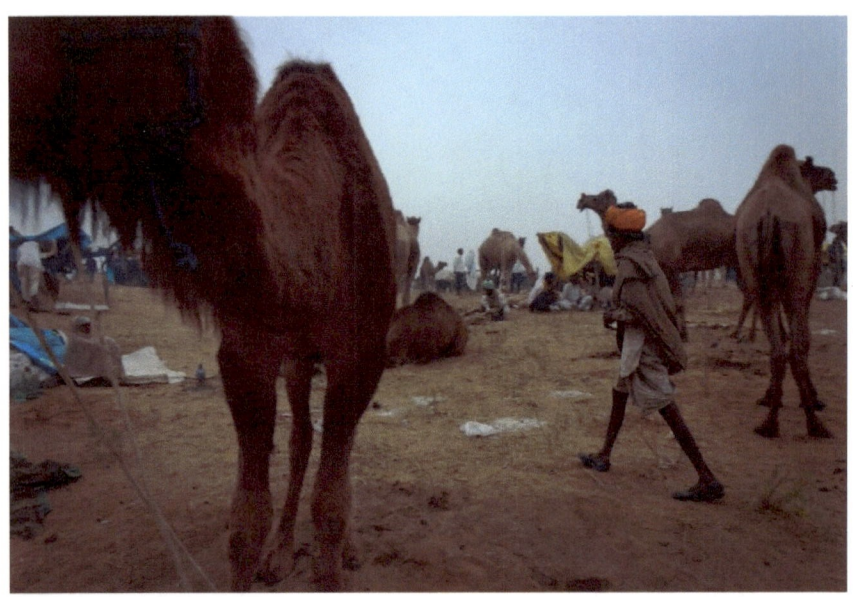

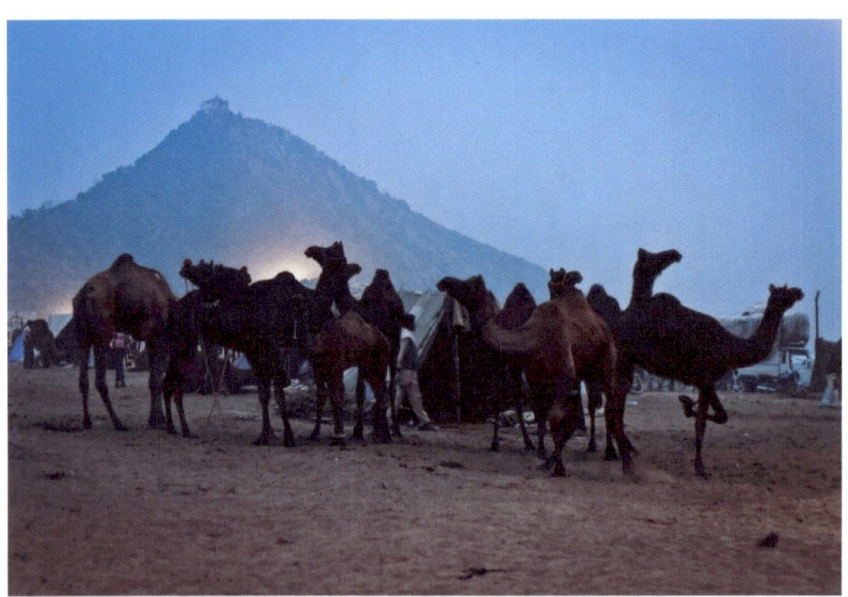

Dusk setting in!

7. COLOURS OF PUSHKAR

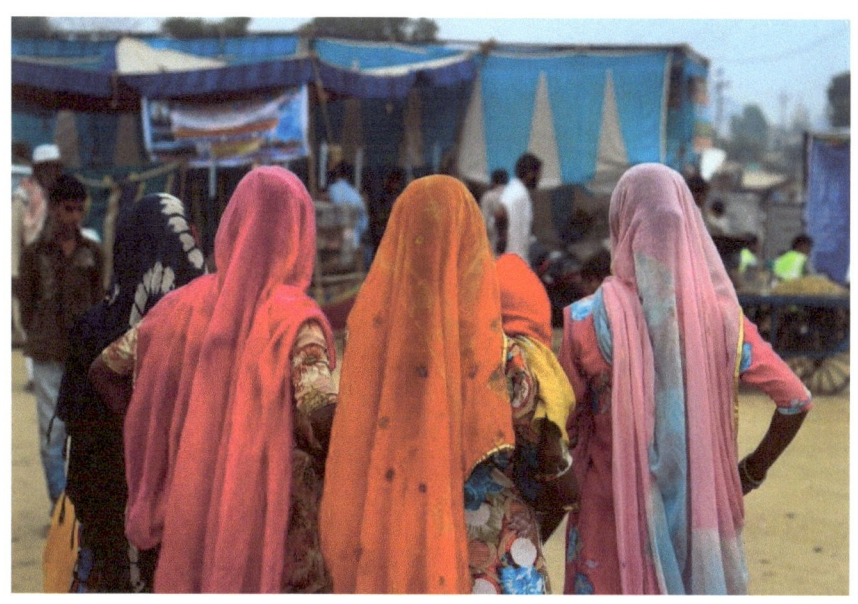

Traditional women dressed in vibrant coloured saaris

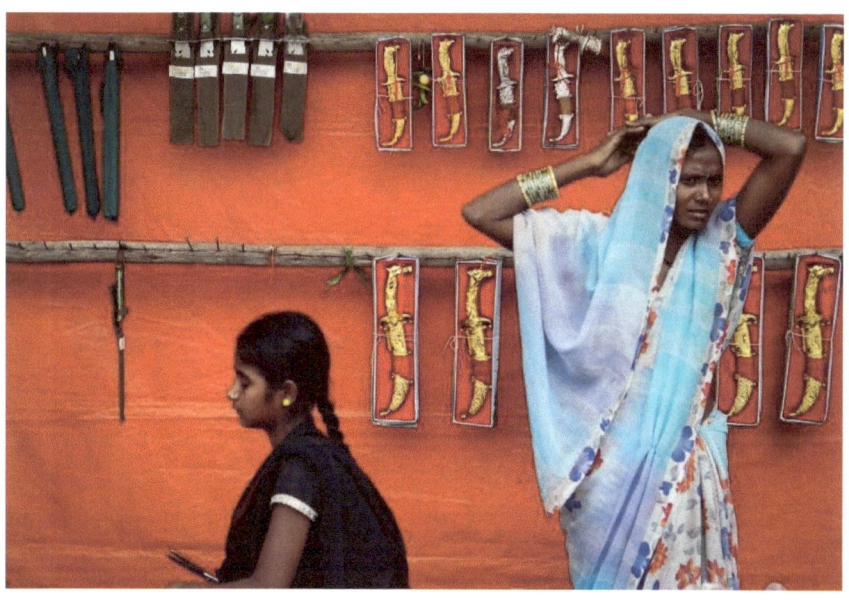

A shop selling daggers and traditional weapons

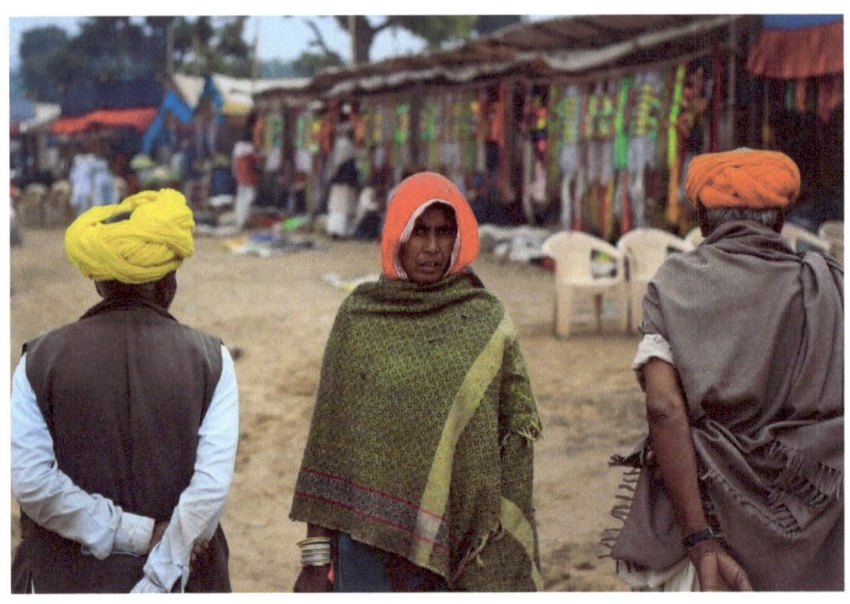

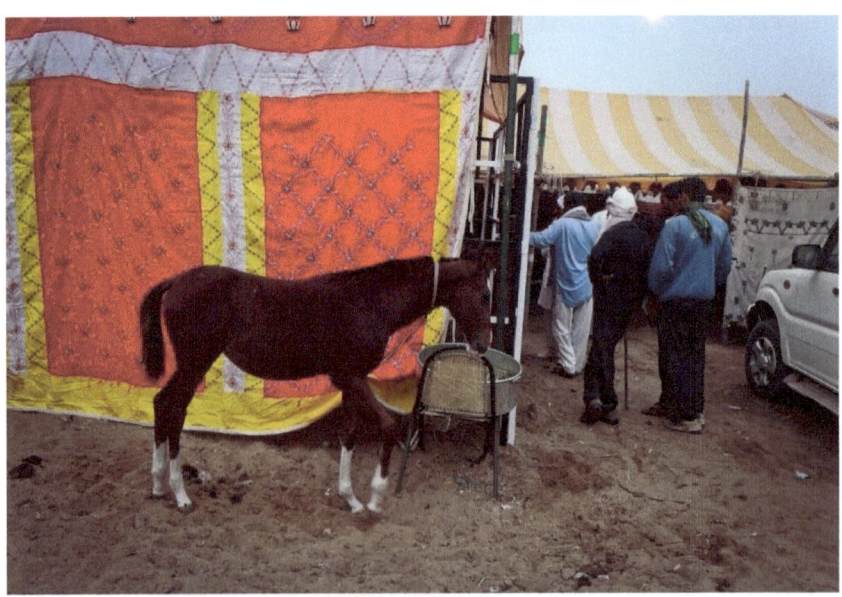

Colours, colours everywhere!

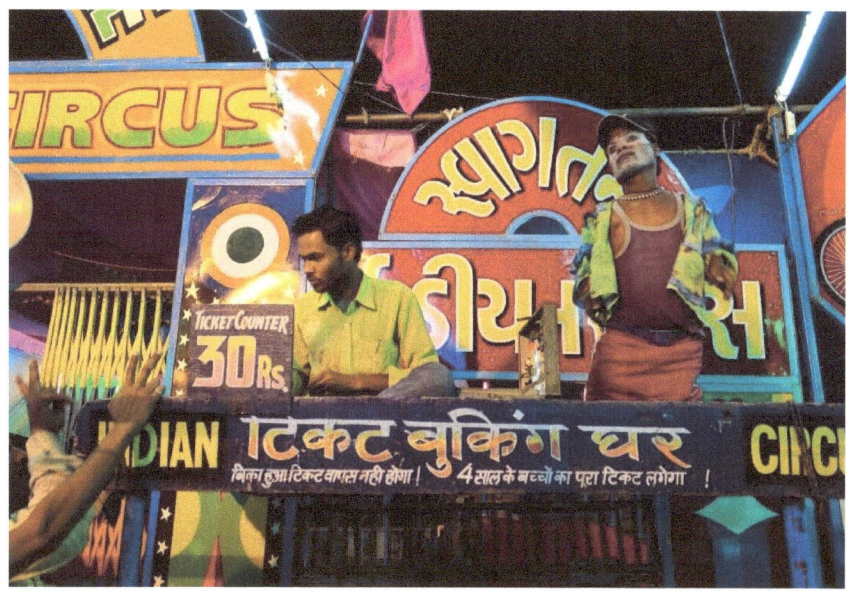

That's the entry gate to the local circus!

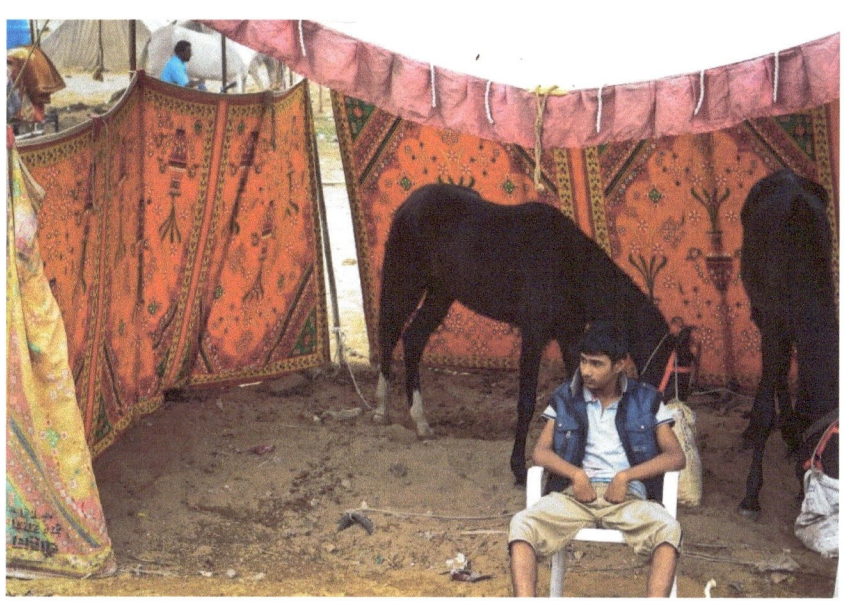

Typical scene at most of the stables

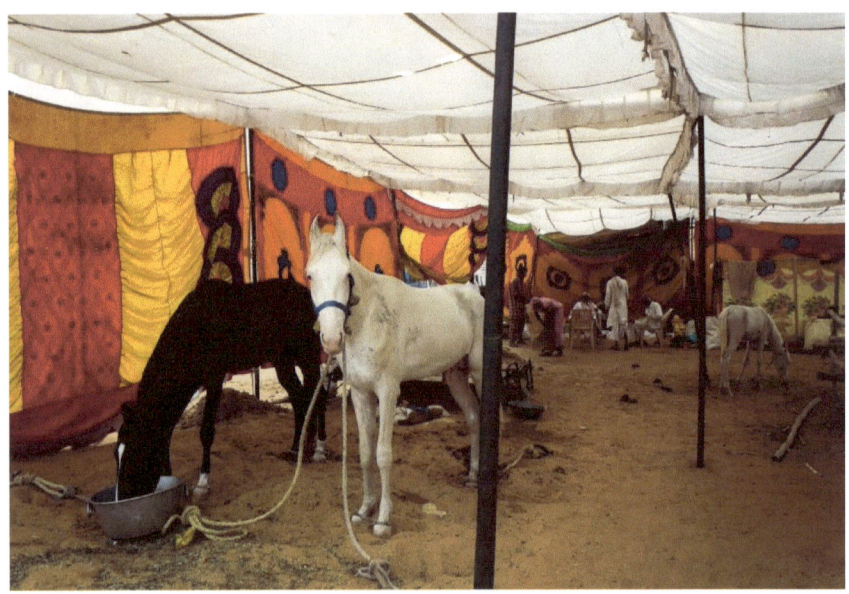

Typical scene at most of the stables

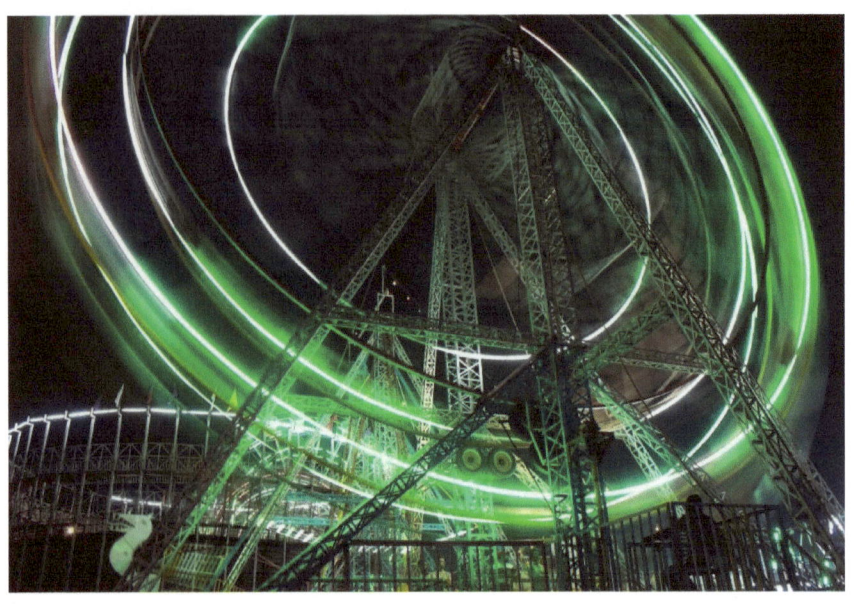

A long exposure shot of the swings

ABOUT THE AUTHOR

Pulkit Joshi is a photography enthusiast who loves to travel and pick up stories through the camera. What started just as a hobby four years back eventually turned into a major passion for him!